LATIN
KEY WORDS

MW00817716

Latin Key Words is a learning aid benefiting from computer analysis of the surviving corpus of Latin literature, comprising over 1,500,000 words. It consists of a list of the most common two thousand words in Latin, with their meanings in English, arranged in decreasing order of frequency. The list is divided into a hundred units of twenty key words each, from which many more words can be derived. All the most common irregular verbs are cited in their full principal parts.

Latin Key Words is the most efficient and logical way to acquire the basic vocabulary of Latin. Most grammars and readers introduce words almost at random, so that a student can never be sure of mastering commonly-occurring words within a reasonable period. A frequency list such as *Latin Key Words* can create confidence and a sense of security in vocabulary building and, by dividing the list into manageable units, mastery can be achieved without undue strain.

Latin Key Words is also weighted towards the authors who appear most often in examinations as set-texts or as the basis for unseen translation. It is therefore of the maximum possible practical benefit for those working towards public examinations.

Dr Jerry Toner has made sure that both adult beginners and school children alike will be introduced to all the most frequently-occurring words in Latin within their first year or two of study. The two thousand key words account for 75% of all word occurrences in Latin. An English index allows the reader to trace each word in the list and indicates by its position the relative frequency of that word.

LATIN
KEY WORDS

the basic 2,000-word vocabulary
arranged by frequency in a
hundred units

with comprehensive Latin and
English indexes

JERRY TONER

The Oleander Press

The Oleander Press
16 Orchard Street
Cambridge
CB1 1JT

Cover image: Annabelle Orozco

CONTENTS

Introduction

It was when I learnt the Latin for 'screech-owl' in my first lesson that I first thought there must be a better way. Some twenty-five years later, I have designed *Latin Key Words* as an efficient, logical and practical computer-based word-list for English-speaking learners of Latin in their first and second year. It is also a valuable revision tool for more advanced students.

The basic two thousand 'key' words are so called because by learning these the student acquires the basic knowledge to open up the whole world of Latin literature but also because they unlock the door to many thousands more words: plurals from singulars, feminines from masculines or neuters, and verb endings from the principal parts.

The purpose of this technique is simply to stimulate confidence in the learning of Latin by beginning with the most common. Nothing is more daunting to the beginner than to face the canon of obscure words that traditionally greeted the learner of Latin (screech- owl was merely the forerunner of such handy words as harpago, grappling hook, mugil, mullet, and vannus, winnowing-fan).

Latin Key Words is intended to be used with a conventional grammar and a conventional dictionary, but a massive dictionary has been found in practice to unnerve the beginner, while most available readers introduce too early words or ideas which may be arbitrary or advanced. At this sensitive phase, where interest in learning Latin can be so easily discouraged, it is suggested that the student should learn words in units of about twenty 'key' words each, thus mastering two thousand such words by the end of the first or second year. Only then will the student be able to accumulate arbitrary words of low occurrence, many of which will in any case be related to words already learnt. Computer-based methods are common to nearly all walks of life now, but statistical sampling has hitherto been rarely practised in language-learning. The Oleander Press pioneered this approach in *French Key Words* by Xavier-Yves Escande, *Italian Key Words* by Gianpaolo Intronati, *Spanish Key Words* by Pedro Casal, *German Key Words* by Dieter Zahn, and *Arabic Key Words* by David Quitregard.

The Units

Each of the hundred units is self-contained, Unit 1 including the twenty most common key words, Unit 2 the next most common and so on. The key word is followed by an indication of its part of speech: *adj.*, adjective; *adv.*, adverb; *conj.*, conjunction; *c.*, common noun; *f.*, feminine noun; *m.*, masculine noun; *n.*, neuter noun; *interj.*, interjection; *num.*, numeral; *part.*, particle *prep.*, preposition; *pron.*, pronoun. Verbs are shown with their principal parts if irregular or if clarity demands. Common alternative forms are given in brackets. Where a verb lacks a principal part a space is left. Deponent verbs are indicated by the abbreviation *dep.*

Many Latin words can be translated by a number of English equivalents. It would be counter-productive, in a work designed to stimulate interest rather than to clog the memory, to list all such equivalents, so only the most common have been cited.

The Indexes

The two indexes permit the reader to use *Latin Key Words* as a basic dictionary, but let it be repeated that a small dictionary should be used in conjunction with this book. A concise and basic grammar should also be used.

Another fascinating usage of the indexes is to discover how frequent and useful each Latin word happens to be. Of course the frequency level applies only to the Latin words: nothing is implied about the relative frequency of their English equivalents. The first 10 words are so common that they account for 16% of total occurrences in a huge lexical universe; the first hundred account for 40%; and the first thousand for 68%. The full 2000 key words represent 75% of all Latin words in a corpus of nearly two million. It is therefore evident that anyone who masters the vocabulary in Latin Key Words is three quarters of the way to mastering the entire corpus of Latin texts.

The Sources

Latin Key Words focuses on the Classical authors favoured by Examination Boards and Universities. It includes the major works of the following authors: Caesar, Catullus, Cicero, Horace, Livy, Ovid, Suetonius, Tacitus, and Virgil. Extra weighting has been given to works according to their frequency of appearance in public examinations in the UK and USA. Extra weighting has also been given to poetry so that the more common poetical words also appear in the list.

Finally, I should like to thank the Oleander Press for giving me this chance to give newcomers to the wonderful Latin language a means of putting the screech-owl behind us all.

Jerry Toner

Principal Parts of Regular Verbs

First Conjugation Ambulare, to walk
| ambulo | ambulare | ambulavi | ambulatum |
| *I walk* | *to walk* | *I walked* | *walked* |

Second Conjugation Habere, to have
| habeo | habere | habui | habitum |
| *I have* | *to have* | *I had* | *had* |

Third Conjugation Regere, to rule
| rego | regere | rexi | rectum |
| *I rule* | *to rule* | *I ruled* | *ruled* |

Fourth Conjugation Audire, to hear
| audio | audire | audivi | auditum |
| *I hear* | *to hear* | *I heard* | *heard* |

First Conjugation Deponent Auxiliari, to help
| auxilior | auxiliari | auxiliatus sum |
| *I help* | *to help* | *I helped* |

Second Conjugation Deponent Vereri, to fear
| vereor | vereri | veritus sum |
| *I fear* | *to fear* | *I feared* |

Third Conjugation Deponent Uti, to use
| utor | uti | usus sum |
| *I use* | *to use* | *I used* |

Fourth Conjugation Deponent Partiri, to divide
| partior | partiri | partitus sum |
| *I divide* | *to divide* | *I divided* |

Unit 1

et *conj.*	and, also
esse	to be
sum esse fui	
qui, quae, quod *pron.*	who, which, what, that
in *prep. + acc. & abl.*	into, in, at
quis, quid *pron.*	who, what
ego *pron.*	I
non *adv.*	not
ut *adv., conj.*	that, so that, as, how
hic, haec, hoc *pron.*	this
tu *pron.*	you
is, ea, id *pron.*	he, she, it
ad *prep. + acc.*	towards, to, near, at
cum *conj., prep. + abl.*	with, when, since
a, ab *prep. + abl.*	from, by
atque, ac *conj.*	and
si *conj.*	if
dicere	to say, speak
dico dicere dixi dictum	
sed *conj.*	but
ille, illa, illud *pron.*	that
de *prep. + abl.*	from, out of, down from, concerning

Unit 2

se, sese   *pron.*   himself, herself, itself
e, ex   *prep. + abl.*   out of, from
neque, nec   *adv., conj.*   not, nor, neither...nor...
facere   to do, make
    facio facere feci factum
posse   to be able to, can
    possum posse potui
aut   *conj.*   or, either...or..., or else
videre   to see
    video videre visi visum
ipse, ipsa, ipsum   *pron.*   himself, herself, itself
res   *f.*   thing, matter, wealth, business
habere   to have, hold
    habeo habere habui
    habitum
etiam   *conj.*   even, yet, indeed
enim   *conj.*   for, indeed
tuus   *pron.*   your
nam   *conj.*   for, indeed
vos   *pron.*   you
per   *prep. + acc,*   through, along, during, by, for
magnus   *adj.*   big, large, great
iam   *adv.*   now, already
ire   to go, proceed
    eo ire ii (ivi) itum
quam   *adv.*   how, what a...!, than

Unit 3

homo *m.*	human being
dare	to give
do dare dedi datum	
hue *adv.*	to this place, hither
velle	to wish, be willing
volo velle volui	
autem *conj.*	however, but
tamen *adv.*	however
multus *adj.*	much, many
nunc *adv.*	now
venire	to come
venio venire veni ventum	
omnis *adj.*	all
pro *prep. + abl.*	before, on behalf of, for, according to
causa *f.*	cause, reason, motive
nihil, nil *adv., n.*	nothing, not at all
meus *pron.*	my, mine
quidem *conj.*	indeed
noster *pron.*	our, ours
agere	to drive, do, make
ago agere egi actum	
tantus *pron.*	so great, so large, of such a kind
nullus *adj.*	none, nobody, no-one
iste, ista, istud *pron.*	that person, that thing

Unit 4

tempus *n.*	time, temple of the head
pars *f.*	part, portion, piece
tum *adv.*	then
idem, eadem, idem *adj.*	the same
nos *pron.*	we
unus *num.*	one
ferre	to bear, carry, bring
fero ferre tuli latum	
alius *adj.*	other, another
illic *adv.*	there
suus *pron.*	his, her, its, theirs
quia *conj.*	because
animus *m.*	soul, spirit
urbs *f*	city
populus *m.*	people
modus *m.*	measure, manner
vel *conj.*, *adv.*	or, actually, or even
senatus *m.*	senate
ita *adv.*	thus, so
pater *m.*	father
sic *adv.*	thus, so

Unit 5

nequeo   to be unable
    nequeo nequire
    nequii (nequivi) nequitum
deus   *m.*   god
reri   *dep.*   to think, consider
    reor reri ratus sum
dies   m.   day
ubi   *adv.*   where
inter   *prep. + acc.*   between, among
ante   *adv., prep. + acc.*   before
quo   *pron.*   where?
fieri   to be made, happen
    fio fieri factus sum
primus   *adj.*   first, foremost
parvus   *adj.*   small, little
apud   *prep. + acc.*   at, near, by, with
hostis   *m.*   stranger, enemy, foreigner
scire   to know
    scio scire scii (scivi) scitum
bonus   *adj.*   good
tam   *adv.*   so much, so far, so
domus   *f.*   house, home, household
accipere   to take, receive, accept
    accipio accipere accepi
    acceptum
putare   to reckon, consider
scribere   to write
    scribo scribere scripsi
    scriptum

Unit 6

at *conj.*	but, yet .moreover
mittere	to send, let go
mitto mittere misi missum	
civitas *f.*	citizenship, state
reficere	to restore, repair
reficio reficere refeci refectum	
audire	to listen, hear
quidam, quaedam, quodam pron., *adj.*	a certain person, thing
littera *f.*	letter, literature
consul *m.*	consul
nomen *n.*	name
certus *adj.*	definite, certain
totus *adj.*	all
credere	to believe, trust
credo credere credidi creditum	
ne *part.*	truly, not, lest (to express a question)
petere	to seek, request, attack
peto petere petii (petivi) petitum	
an *conj.*	whether
quisquam, quaequam, quidquam pron., *adj.*	anybody, anything
locus *m.*	place, situation, location
iubere	to order, command
iubeo iubere iussi iussum	
bellum *n.*	war
verus *adj*	true, real

Unit 7

quisque, quaeque, quidque
    pron.   each, every

post   *adv., prep. + acc.*   behind, after

sequi   *dep.*   to follow, pursue
    sequor sequi secutus sum

vis   *f.*   force, power

potis   *adj.*   powerful, capable

verbum   *n.*   word

amare   to love

vir   *m.*   man, husband

consilium   *n.*   counsel, council

tenere   to hold, grasp
    teneo tenere tenui tentum

modo   *adv.*   only, alone, but, just

redire   to go back, return
    redeo redire redii (redivi)
    reditum

debere   to owe
    debeo debere debui
    debitum

manus   *f.*   hand

duo   *num.*   two

dum   *conj.*   while, until

longus   *adj.*   long

ratio   *f.*   account, reason, business

miles   *c.*   soldier

quaerere   to seek
    quaero quaerere
    quaesii (quaesivi) quaesitum

Unit 8

alter *adj.*	one of two, the other one
terra *f.*	land, earth
vester *pron.*	your, yours
iudicium *n.*	trial, judgment, opinion
aiere (defective verb)	to say yes, assent
ius *n.*	law, right
filius *m.*	son
relinquere	to leave behind, abandon
relinquo relinquere	
reliqui relictum	
referre	to bring back, report
refero referre retuli	
relatum	
vocare	to call
ponere	to put, place, locate
pono ponere posui	
positum	
contra *adv., prep. + acc.*	opposite, against
virtus *f.*	manly excellence, virtue,
courage	
annus *m.*	year
publicus *adj.*	public
quin *conj.*	why not, so that not
capere	to take, seize
capio capere cepi captum	
opus *n.*	work
niti *dep.*	to push, strain
nitor niti nixus sum	
stare	to stand
sto stare steti statum	

Unit 9

provincia *f.*	province, office
corpus *n.*	body
intellegere	to understand
intellego intellegere	
intellexi intellectum	
lex *f*	law
imperium *n.*	command, power, authority
uti *dep.*	to use
utor uti usus sum	
legio *f.*	legion
ergo *adv.*	therefore
propter *adv., prep. + acc.*	near, because of
quasi *adv.*	as if
spes *f.*	hope
igitur *adv.*	therefore
civis *c.*	citizen
superus *adj.*	higher, upper
deinde, dein *adv.*	then, thereupon
semper *adv.*	always
amicus *m., adj.*	friend, friendly
gerere	to carry, wear
gero gerere gessi gestum	
adeo *adv.*	so far, so long, even
nisi *conj.*	if not, unless, except

Unit 10

simul *adv.*	at the same time
periculum *n.*	danger
rex *m.*	king
legare	to bequeath, appoint as envoy
nemo *c.*	no-one, nobody
iudicare	to judge, decide
quantus *adj.*	how great, how much
mors *f.*	death
ullus *adj.*	any
aliquis, aliqua, aliquid *pron.*	someone, something, anyone, anything
loqui *dep.*	to speak
loquor loqui locutus sum	
cognoscere	to know, learn about
cognosco cognoscere	
cognovi cognitum	
ager *m.*	field
dedere	to give up, surrender, devote
dedo dedere dedidi deditum	
tribunus *m.*	tribune
prior *adj.*	first, prior
nox *f.*	night
pecunia *f.*	money
sub *prep. + abl. & acc.*	under, beneath
mater *f.*	mother

Unit 11

facilis *adj.*	easy
hinc *adv.*	from here, hence
amor *m.*	love
sive, seu *conj.*	or if, whether
frater *m.*	brother
haud *adv.*	not at all, not
valere valeo valere valui	to be healthy, prevail

consulere
    consulo consulere
    consului consultum
	to deliberate, consult

sinere sino sinere sivi situm	to permit, allow
numquam *adv.*	never
vivere vivo vivere vixi victum	to live
vita *f.*	life
malus *adj.*	bad, evil
adesse adsum adesse adfui	to be present, be at

ostendere
    ostendo ostendere
    ostendi ostensum
	to show, display

arma *n. pl.*	weapons, tools
sanus *adj.*	healthy, sound
gratia *f.*	grace, favour, goodwill
gens *f.*	people, tribe, nation

sentire
    sentio sentire sensi
    sensum
	to perceive, feel, sense

Unit 12

solus *adj.*	sole, only
gravis *adj.*	heavy, serious
sententia *f.*	thought, opinion, feeling
rus *n.*	country, countryside
reddere	to give back, restore
reddo reddere reddidi redditum	
oculus *m.*	eye
uter, utra, utrum *pron.*	each of two, both
studium *n.*	zeal, enthusiasm
movere	to move
moveo movere movi motum	
pati *dep.*	to suffer, endure
patior pati passus sum	
defendere	to defend, repel
defendo defendere defendi defensum	
ob *prep. + acc.*	towards, because of
fortis *adj.*	strong, powerful
vox *f.*	voice
factum *n.*	deed
reus *m.*	defendant
armare	to equip, arm
curare	to care for; tend
fortuna *f.*	fortune, luck, chance
ibi *adv.*	there

Unit 13

pax *f.*	peace
appellere	to drive, call, address
appello appellere	
appuli appulsum	
abire	to go away
abeo abire abii (abivi)	
abitum	
fides *f.*	faith, trust, belief
genus *n.*	birth, nation, race, kind
vero *adv.*	in truth, truly
vincere	to conquer
vinco vincere vici victum	
parare	to prepare, purchase
plebs *f.*	the common people, the masses
aetas *f.*	age
aurum *n.*	gold, money
cur *adv.*	why
negare	to deny
iudex *m.*	judge
auctoritas *f.*	authority, influence
ordo *m.*	line, row, order
fama *f.*	talk, rumour, reputation, fame
mos *m.*	habit, custom, character
tempestas *f*.	season, weather, storm
solere	to be accustomed to, be used to
soleo solere solitus sum	

Unit 14

invenire	to find, discover, invent
invenio invenire inveni inventum	
quisquis, quaequae, quidquid *pron.*	whoever
legere	to collect, select, read
lego legere legi lectum	
copia *f.*	supply, abundance
puer *m.*	boy, son
dux c.	leader
perire	to pass away, die
pereo perire perii (perivi) peritum	
quoniam *conj.*	since, whereas, because
ferrum *n.*	iron, sword
malum *n.*	evil
afferre	to bring to, carry to
affero afferre attuli allatum	
cogere	to bring together, collect, compel
cogo cogere coegi coactum	
tradere	to hand over, relate, betray
trado tradere tradidi traditum	
potestas *f.*	power
cura *f.*	care, worry, trouble
exercere	to exercise, train
exerceo exercere exercui exercitum	
respondere	to respond, answer
respondeo respondere respondi responsum	
metus *m.*	fear, dread
aqua f.	water
dignitas *f.*	esteem, rank, status, worth

Unit 15

tollere	to lift up, take away, raise
tollo tollere sustuli sublatum	
nolle	to be unwilling, do not wish
nolo nolle nolui	
honor *m.*	honour, public office
abesse	to be absent, be away
absum abesse abfui	
uxor *f.*	wife
magis *adv.*	more, rather
oratio *f.*	speech, speaking
princeps *adj.*	prince, leader
oportet	it ought, it is right to
multo *adv.*	by much, greatly
salus *f.*	health, safety
fugere	to run away, flee
fugio to fear, be afraid	
timere	to fear, be afraid
timeo timere timui	
existimare	to evaluate, judge, consider
bene *adv.*	well
constituere	to place, locate, found
constituo constituere constitui constitutum	
signum *n.*	mark, sign, seal
crimen *n.*	accusation, crime
constare	to stop, exist, remain
consto constare constiti constatum	
caput *n.*	head, top

Unit 16

tueri *dep.*	to look at, guard
tueor tueri tutus sum	
rogare	to ask
sicut *adv.*	just as
novus *adj.*	new, novel, strange
regere	to rule, direct
rego regere rexi rectum	
que *conj.*	and
servare	to watch over, observe
quoque *adv.*	also, too
miser *adj.*	poor, wretched, sad
locare	to place, locate
recipere	to take back, draw back, receive
recipio recipere recepi receptum	
noscere	to get to know, recognise
nosco noscere novi notum	
ideo *adv.*	on that account, therefore
diu *adv.*	for a long time
exercitus *m.*	army
mons *m.*	mountain
numerus *m.*	number
dolor *n.*	pain, sorrow
natura *f.*	origin, nature
fari *dep.*	to speak, say
for fari fatus sum	

Unit 17

umquam *adv.*	ever, at any time
placeo	please
placeo placere placui placitum	
eques *m.*	horseman, cavalryman, knight
ceterus *adj.*	the other, the rest
templum *n.*	temple
praetor *m.*	praetor
mille *num.*	thousand
equus. *m.*	horse
ingens *adj.*	huge, grand, vast
cedere	proceed, withdraw, yield
cedo cedere cessi cessum	
postea *adv.*	afterwards, next
talis *adj.*	of such a kind
praesidium *n.*	guard, protection, security
cadere	to fall
cado cadere cecidi	
convenire	to come together, agree
convenio convenire conveni conventum	
denique *adv.*	finally, at last
mens *f.*	mind, reason
tres *num.*	three
pectus *n.*	chest
castra *n. pl.*	camp, fort

Unit 18

gratus *adj.*	agreeable, kind, grateful
vertere	to turn, rotate, change
verto vertere versi versum	
censere	to think, reckon
censeo censere censui censum	
finis *c.*	boundary, limit, end
cupere	to desire, want
cupio cupere cupii (cupivi) cupitum	
accedere	to approach
accedo accedere accessi accessum	
probare	to try, test, approve
laudare	to praise
sol *m.*	sun
maximus *adj.*	greatest, largest, maximum
opera *f.*	work, effort
sumere	to take
sumo sumere sumpsi sumptum	
perdere	to lose
perdo perdere perdidi perditum	
exspectare	to wait for, expect
ingenium *n.*	character, nature, talent
coepere	to begin
coepio coepere coepi coeptum	
sperare	to hope
poena *f.*	punishment, penalty
postquam *adv.*	after
iter *n.*	journey

Unit 19

audere	to dare
audeo audere ausus sum	
sanguis *m.*	blood, bloodshed
victoria *f.*	victory, conquest
hodie *adv.*	today
aedes *f.*	temple
navis *f.*	ship, boat
usque *adv., prep. + acc.*	at every point, as far as, constantly
ignis *m.*	fire
divus *adj.*	divine
laus *f.*	praise
ira *f.*	anger
postulare	to ask for, demand, beg
pugnare	to fight
ducere	to draw, lead
duco ducere duxi ductum	
orare	to pray, speak, beg
tot *num.*	so many
adhuc *adv.*	to this point, hitherto, thus far
fors *n.*	chance, luck
alere	to nourish, support
alo alere alui altum (alitum)	
dubitare	to doubt, hesitate

Unit 20

filia *f.*	daughter
manere	to stay, remain
maneo manere mansi mansum	
officium *n.*	duty, service, office
multitudo *f.*	multitude, large number
servus *m., adj.*	slave, servile, slavish
vix *adv.*	hardly, scarcely
litus *n.*	sea-shore
exire	to go out, die
exeo exire exii (exivi) exitum	
ops *f.*	power, wealth
nasci *dep.*	to be born
nascor nasci natus sum	
tegere	to cover, conceal, protect
tego tegere texi tectum	
via *f.*	road, way
significare	to signify, indicate
concedere	to withdraw, concede
concedo concedere concessi concessum	
mori *dep.*	to die
morior mori mortuus sum	
libertas *f.*	liberty, freedom
praeter *adv.*	more than, beyond
amplus *adj.*	large, ample
mox *adv.*	soon
docere	to teach
doceo docere docui doctum	

Unit 21

malle malo malle malui	to prefer
senex *m., adj.*	old man, old
flumen *n.*	river
cogitare	to think, consider
validus *adj.*	strong, healthy, powerful
epistula *f.*	letter
oppidum *n.*	town
tacere taceo tacere tacui tacitum	to be silent, be quiet

subire
   subeo subire subii (subivi)
   subitum
	to go under

deesse desum deesse defui	to be absent, be lacking, fail
fallere fallo fallere fefelli falsum	to deceive, trick
labor *m.*	work, toil
voluntas *f.*	will, wish
agmen *n.*	crowd, mass
scilicet *adv.*	actually, certainly, namely
statim *adv.*	at once
regnum *n.*	sovereignty, tyranny, realm
clarus *adj.*	clear, bright, famous

decernere
   decerno decernere decrevi
   decretum
	to decide

imperator *m.*	general, emperor

Unit 22

dignus   *adj.* — worthy, deserving

religio   *f.* — religion, reverence, superstition

edere — to give out, bring forth, produce
   edo edere edidi editum

inimicus   *adj.* — unfriendly, hostile

itaque   *adv.* — therefore

patrius   *adj.* — fatherly

sine   *prep. + abl.* — without

iuvenis   *adj.* — young

medius   *adj.* — middle, central

negotium   *n.* — work, business

praeda   *f.* — booty, plunder, loot

deferre — to bring down, transport
   defero deferre detuli delatum

acies   *f.* — edge, battle line, piercing look

reliquus   *adj.* — rest, remainder

colere — to live in, cultivate
   colo colere colui cultum

gloria   *f.* — glory, fame

spectare — to look at, watch

gener   *m.* — son-in-law

mulier   *f.* — woman, wife

advenire — to arrive
   advenio advenire adveni adventum

Unit 23

volvere
    volvo volvere volui
    volutum
	to turn, roll

comparare	to compare

conferre
    confero conferre contuli
    collatum
	to bring together, hire, serve

metuere
    metuo metuere metui
    metutum
	to fear

diligere diligo diligere dilexi dilectum	to prize, love

efficere
    efficio efficere effeci
    effectum
	to make, effect, accomplish

summus *adj.*	highest
posterus *adj.*	next, following
prope *adv., prep. + acc.*	close, near
victor *m.*	conqueror
silva *f.*	wood, forest
pugna *f.*	fight, battle

caedere
    caedo caedere cecidi
    caesum
	to strike, cut down, kill

scelus *n.*	crime, evil
munus *n.*	office, duty, present, gift
impetus *m.*	attack, force
proelium *n.*	battle, fight
soror *f.*	sister
etsi *conj.*	although, yet

amittere
    amitto amittere amisi
    amissum
	to send away, dismiss

statuere
    statuo statuere statui
    statutum
	to place, locate, establish

Unit 24

trahere	to drag, pull
traho trahere traxi tractum	
inde *adv.*	from there, thence, then
tunc *adv.*	then
odium *n.*	hatred
auctor *m.*	author, maker
similis *adj.*	like, similar
discedere	to depart, disperse
discedo discedere discessi	
discessum	
tandem *adv.*	at last, finally
levis *adj.*	light, quick, trifling
quando *adv., conj.*	when
argentum *n.*	silver, money
velut *adv.*	just as, as if
numen *n.*	nod, divine will
mutare	to change, alter
virgo *f.*	virgin, maiden
ornare	to prepare, decorate
retinere	to hold back, restrain
retineo retinere retinui	
retentum	
licet	it is permitted
vitare	to avoid
beneficium *n.*	favour, benefit

Unit 25

imperare	to order, command
equidem *part.*	indeed
parere	to obey, be apparent
pareo parere parui paritum	
inferre	to carry in, infer
infero inferre intuli illatum	
reperire	to find
reperio reperire	
reperi (repperi) repertum	
vetus *adj.*	old, ancient
cohors *f.*	cohort
vultus *m.*	expression, face
pertinere	to relate, pertain to
pertineo pertinere pertinui	
proficisci *dep.*	to set out, depart
proficiscor proficisci	
profectus sum	
nobilis *adj.*	well-known, remarkable, noble
sero *adv.*	late, too late
eripere	to tear away
eripio eripere eripui ereptum	
transire	to go beyond, pass over
transeo transire	
transii (transivi) transitum	
familia *f.*	household
tamquam *adv.*	just as, as if
vulnus *n.*	wound, injury
augere	to increase, grow
augeo augere auxi auctum	
auferre	to carry away, remove
aufero auferre abstuli	
ablatum	
classis *f.*	class, fleet

Unit 26

nominare	to name, nominate, make famous
sustinere	to support; sustain
sustineo sustinere sustinui	
certamen *n.*	contest, struggle, fight
usus *m.*	use, practice
natus *m.*	birth
pervenire	to arrive, reach
pervenio pervenire perveni perventum	
liber *adj.*	free
nuntiare	to announce
turbare	to disturb, confuse
fuga *f.*	flight
turbo *f.*	whirlpool, whirlwind
foedus *adj.*	foul, filthy, disgraceful
praesens *adj.*	present, in person, immediate
liceri *dep.*	to bid for
liceor liceri licitus sum	
solvere	to set loose, release, break up
solvo solvere solvi solutum	
oriri *dep.*	to rise
orior oriri ortus sum	
prohibere	to prohibit, hold back
prohibo prohibere prohibui prohibitum	
occidere	to cut down, kill
occido occidere occidi occisum	
militare	to be a soldier
necesse *adj.*	necessary

Unit 27

telum *n.*	spear, weapon
amicitia *f.*	friendship
continere	to keep together, retain,
contineo continere continui	maintain
contentum	
excipere	to take out, receive
excipio excipere excepi	
exceptum	
potare	to drink
aequus *adj.*	level, equal, fair
consulatus *m.*	consulship
contendere	to strive
contendo contendere	
contendi contentum	
invidia *f.*	hate, envy
quicumque, quaecumque,	
quodcumque *pron.*	whoever, whatever
sacer *adj.*	holy, sacred
adducere	to lead to, bring to
adduco adducere adduxi	
adductum	
saxum *n.*	rock, stone
murus *m.*	wall, fortification
accidere	to fall, befall, happen
accido accidere accidi	
committere	to bring together, unite
committo committere	
commisi commissum	
populare	to plunder, devastate
liberare	to set free, liberate
suscipere	to undertake
suscipio suscipere suscepi	
susceptum	
aperire	to open, uncover
aperio aperire aperui	
apertum	

Unit 28

contio *f.*	public, assembly
socius m., *adj.*	ally, partner, allied
auris *f.*	ear
poscere	to ask for, demand
posco poscere poposci	
secundus *adj.*	following, second
memoria *f.*	memory, tradition
familiaris *adj.*	the household's, familiar
indicere	to proclaim, announce
indico indicere indixi	
indictum	
laborare	to work
proficere	to advance, be of use
proficio proficere profeci	
profectum	
currere	to run
curro currere cucurri	
cursum	
campus *m.*	plain, field
quaeso *(fixed form of verb)*	I beg you, please
gaudere	to rejoice
gaudeo gaudere	
gavisus sum	
nescire	to be ignorant of
nescio nescire	
nescii (nescivi) nescitum	
vereri *dep.*	to fear
vereor vereri veritus sum	
vetare	to forbid, prevent
veto vetare vetui vetitum	
instituere	to arrange, establish
instituo instituere institui	
institutum	
acer *adj.*	sharp
tangere	to touch
tango tangere tetigi tactum	

Unit 29

accusare	to accuse
genu *n.*	knee
frumentum *n.*	grain
solum *adv.*	only, alone
anima *f.*	wind, spirit, soul
forum *n.*	market-place, forum
adulescens *adj., m.*	adolescent, youth
vellere	to pluck
vello vellere vulsi (velli) vulsum	
merere	to earn, deserve
mereo merere merui meritum	
antea *adv.*	before, formerly
tertius *adj.*	third
creare	to create, produce
clamor *m.*	shout, cry
dictator *m.*	dictator, commander
memini, meminisse *(perfect forms only)*	to remember
timor *m.*	fear, dread
visere	to visit
viso visere visi visum	
caedes *f.*	slaughter
cunctus *adj.*	all
exemplum *n.*	sample, example

Unit 30

praemium *n.*	reward, prize, profit
optare	to choose, select
perficere	to finish, perfect, accomplish
perficio perficere perfeci perfectum	
rapere	to seize, snatch
rapio rapere rapui raptum	
omnino *adv.*	altogether, entirely
plenus *adj.*	full, complete
deducere	to lead away, bring down
deduco deducere deduxi deductum	
patria *f.*	homeland, country
signare	to sign, signify
consuetudo *f.*	custom, habit
magistratus *m.*	magistrate
species *f.*	sight, species
procul *adv.*	at a distance, far away
honestus *adj.*	honourable, glorious
libet	it is pleasing
unda *f.*	wave
caelum *n.*	sky, heavens
iacere	to lie, recline
iaceo iacere iacui	
puella *f.*	girl, daughter
integer *adj.*	whole, entire, unharmed

Unit 31

olim *adv.* — once upon a time, someday
legatus *m.* — ambassador, legate
par *adj.* — equal, like
paucus *adj.* — little, few
porta *f.* — gate
alienus *adj.* — strange, unrelated
eodem *adv.* — to the same place, just so far
spatium *n.* — space
iuvare — to help, aid
   iuvo iuvare iuvi iutum
praesertim *adv.* — especially
paene *adv.* — nearly, almost
mandare — to entrust, order
antiquus *adj.* — old, ancient
ferus *adj.* — wild
dimittere — to send away, dismiss
   dimitto dimittere dimisi
   dimissum
quivis *pron.* — whoever, whatever
sus *c.* — pig
iungere — to join
   iungo iungere iunxi
   iunctum
condicio *f.* — agreement, contract
fingere — to mould, shape, create
   fingo fingere finxi fictum

Unit 32

testis *c.*	witness
lacrima *f.*	tear, weeping
privare	to deprive of
vestis *f.*	clothes, clothing
improbus *adj.*	bad, wrong, enormous
magnitudo *f.*	size, magnitude, greatness
omittere	to omit, let go
omitto omittere omisi omissum	
superare	to be over, conquer, dominate
praeterea *adv.*	besides
collega *m.*	colleague
ars *f.*	skill, craft, art
incipere	to begin
incipio incipere incepi inceptum	
premere	to press, crush
premo premere pressi pressum	
portus *m.*	port, harbour
aspicere	to look at, behold
aspicio aspicere aspexi aspectum	
lux *f.*	light, daylight
monere	to advise, warn
moneo monere monui monitum	
quinque *num.*	five
revertere	to turn around, return
reverto revertere reverti reversum	
advertere	to turn towards, direct
adverto advertere adverti adversum	

Unit 33

artus *m.*	limb, leg
irasci *dep.*	to be angry
irascor irasci iratus sum	
cernere	to see, discern
cerno cernere crevi cretum	
laetus *adj.*	happy
occupare	to occupy, take possession of
sex *num.*	six
ardere	to burn, glow
ardeo ardere arsi arsum	
donare	to donate, present
frons *f.*	forehead, brow, front
restituere	to restore
restituo restituere restitui restitutum	
certare	to compete, struggle for
vendere	to sell
vendo vendere vendidi venditum	
dexter *adj.*	right
tabula *f.*	board, table, writing tablet
fateri *dep.*	to admit, confess
fateor fateri fassus sum	
iniuria *f.*	injury, injustice
regnare	to rule, reign
dubius *adj.*	uncertain, doubtful
coniungere	to join together, marry
coniungo coniungere coniunxi coniunctum	
evenire	to come out, happen
evenio evenire eveni eventum	

Unit 34

interesse
    intersum interesse interfui
    to be between, be different

novare
    to renew

impedire
    to impede, block

repetere
    repeto repetere
    repetii (repetivi) repetitum
    to go again, demand again

servire
    servio servire servii (servivi)
    servitum
    to serve

mare *n.*
    sea

pellere
    pello pellere pepuli
    pulsum
    to strike, knock, drive away

publicare
    to make public, publish

insula *f.*
    island, apartment block

os (*gen.* oris) *n.*
    mouth, face

promittere
    promitto promittere promisi
    promissum
    to send ahead, promise

sapere
    sapio sapere sapii
    to perceive, discern

dea *f.*
    goddess

miscere
    misceo miscere miscui
    mixtum
    to mix

obsecrare
    to beseech, beg for

queri *dep.*
    queror queri questus sum
    to complain

salvus *adj.*
    safe, healthy

primo *adv.*
    at first, in the beginning

fundere
    fundo fundere fudi fusum
    to pour

pudor *m.*
    shame

Unit 35

remittere
   remitto remittere remisi
   remissum
	to send back, release

tendere
   tendo tendere tetendi
   tentum
	to stretch, strive

carmen *n.*	song, poem
ventus *m.*	wind
damnare	to convict, condemn
morari *dep.*	to delay, linger
placare	to soothe, placate
patere pateo patere patui	to be open

perferre
   perfero perferre pertuli
   perlatum
	to carry through, complete

arbor *f.*	tree
saepe *adv.*	often
confirmare	to confirm, establish
libido *f.*	lust, desire
nondum *adv.*	not yet
aliter *adv.*	otherwise
communis *adj.*	public, common, general

exigere
   exigo exigere exegi
   exactum
	to drive out, exact

parens *c., adj.*	parent, obedient
auxilium *n.*	help
intro *adv.*	within

Unit 36

regio *f.*	line, boundary, region
cupiditas *f.*	desire, ambition
narrare	to tell, relate, narrate
recens *adj.*	new, fresh, recent
opinari *dep.*	to think, consider
proprius *adj.*	one's own, personal, peculiar
expedire	to set free, provide,
expedio expedire	be expedient
expedii (expedivi) expeditum	
iussum *n.*	command, order
foris *f.*	door
inducere	to lead in, persuade, induce
induco inducere induxi	
inductum	
quondam *adv.*	once upon a time
supplicium *n.*	entreaty, penalty, punishment
donec *conj.*	as long as, until, while
fatum *m.*	fate, destiny
somnus *m.*	sleep
casus *m.*	fall, accident, event
lumen *n.*	light
deserere	to desert
desero deserere deserui	
desertum	
interea *adv.*	meanwhile
errare	to wander, be wrong

Unit 37

tergum *n.*	back
ludus *m.*	game, sport
voluptas *f.*	desire, pleasure
terror *m.*	fear, terror
altus *adj.*	high, deep
cavere	to be careful, beware
caveo cavere cavi cautum	
facinus *n.*	crime
sedere	to sit, stay
sedeo sedere sedi sessum	
fidere	to trust, believe
fido fidere fisus sum	
habitare	to inhabit, dwell
iterum *adv.*	again
quire	to be able, can
queo quire quii (quivi)	
quitum	
obtinere	to hold, maintain
obtineo obtinere obtinui	
obtentum	
salutare	to greet, hail
paulus *adj.*	small, little
memorare	to remember, recount
dominus *m.*	master
memor *adj.*	mindful, thoughtful
iurare	to swear, take an oath
pulcher *adj.*	beautiful

Unit 38

opinio *f*.	opinion, belief
summa *f*.	peak, summit
consularis *adj.*	consular
regius *adj.*	royal, regal
comitium *n.*	voting assembly
etenim *conj.*	namely, truly
invitus *adj.*	unwilling
centurio *m.*	centurion
commendare	to entrust, recommend
frangere	to break
frango frangere fregi fractum	
lingua *f*.	tongue, speech, language, dialect
opprimere	to oppress, subdue
opprimo opprimere oppressi oppressum	
proferre	to bring forth, reveal, advance
profero proferre protuli prolatum	
imago *f.*	image, statue, painting
rursus *adv.*	again
revocare	to recall
furor *m.*	madness, rage
sors *f.*	lot, fate
domare	to subdue, dominate
domo domare domui domitum	
inire	to enter
ineo inire inii (inivi) initum	

Unit 39

nocere noceo nocere nocui	to harm, injure
optimus *adj.*	best
paulum *adv.*	by a little
facies *f.*	appearance, face

praebere
   praebeo praebere praebui
   praebitum
	to offer, provide

quintus *adj.*	fifth
iactare	to hurl, throw
latitudo *f.*	breadth
saevus *adj.*	savage, wild

commovere
   commoveo commovere
   commovi commotum
	to arouse, disturb

nummus *m.*	coin, money
sacerdos *c.*	priest, priestess

ignoscere
   ignosco ignoscere ignovi
   ignotum
	to pardon, overlook

condere
   condo condere condidi
   conditum
	to establish, found, hide

fax *f.*	torch
intrare	to enter

afficere
   afficio afficere affeci
   affectum
	to affect, do something to

praedicare	to proclaim, tell
conari *dep.*	to try
impetrare	to get, obtain, accomplish

Unit 40

imponere
    impono imponere imposui
    impositum
	to put, set, place

interim *adv.*	meanwhile

procedere
    procedo procedere processi
    processum
	to proceed, happen

iustus *adj.*	just, justifiable, justified
medium *n.*	middle
prex *f.*	request, entreaty, prayer
audacia *f.*	courage, boldness
fugare	to rout, put to flight

contemnere
    contemno contemnere
    contempsi contemptum
	to despise, ridicule

hospes *m.*	host, guest, stranger, foreigner
insidiae *f. pl.*	trap, ambush
moenia *n. pl.*	fortifications
molestus *adj.*	annoying, troublesome

praeterire
    praetereo praeterire
    praeterii (praeterivi)
    praeteritum
	to pass by, omit

proximus *adj.*	nearest

adhibere
    adhibeo adhibere adhibui
    adhibitum
	to bring together, join, supply

pecus *n.*	herd, flock

conficere
    conficio conficere confeci
    confectum
	to do, finish

necessarius *adj.*	necessary, unavoidable
praesto *adv.*	ready at hand, present

Unit 41

sidus *n.*	star
verrere	to sweep
verro verrere verri versum	
carus *adj.*	dear
sacrare	to sanctify, consecrate
crudelis *adj.*	cruel
dolere	to suffer
doleo dolere dolui	
figere	to fix, fasten
figo figere fixi fixum	
aequor *n.*	flat surface, sea, plain
nimius *adj.*	too great, excessive
quattuor *num.*	four
erga *prep. + acc.*	towards, in relation to
vitium *n.*	fault, vice
averto	to turn away, avert
averto avertere averti aversum	
contingere	to touch, happen
contingo contingere contigi contactum	
versare	to turn
libare	to pour, taste
incidere	to fall on, rush, occur
incido incidere incidi incasum	
ara *f.*	altar
instare	to stand on, press upon, pursue
insto instare institi	
flamma *f.*	flame

Unit 42

transferre
    transfero transferre transtuli
    translatum
	to transfer

fidus *adj.*	faithful, trustworthy
colonia *f.*	estate, colony

tribuere
    tribuo tribere tribui
    tributum
	to allot, grant

aer *m.*	air
bis *adv.*	twice
canere cano canere cecini cantum	to sing
indignus *adj.*	unworthy, shameful
decet	it is fitting, appropriate
extremum *n.*	extreme, end
custos *c.*	guard
hasta *f.*	spear
poeta *m.*	poet
arx *f.*	citadel, fortress
vulgus *n.*	the people, the public, the mob
societas *f.*	society, association

deligere
    deligo deligere delegi
    delectum
	to choose, select

honorare	to honour, dignify
auspicium *n.*	divination
initium *n.*	start, beginning

Unit 43

iuxta *adv.*	near, close to
exponere	to set out, expose
expono exponere exposui expositum	
ludere	to play
ludo ludere lusi lusum	
praestare	to excel
praesto praestare praestiti praestitum	
necessitas *f.*	necessity, need
sancire	to ratify, sanction
sancio sancire sanxi sanctum	
turpis *adj.*	foul, shameful
culpa *f.*	blame, fault
fons *m.*	spring
sonare	to sound, resound
sono sonare sonui sonitum	
femina *f.*	woman, female
iacere	to throw
iacio iacere ieci iactum	
disciplina *f.*	training, discipline
pes *m.*	foot
dividere	to divide, separate
divido dividere divisi divisum	
quippe *conj.*	indeed, for sure
egredi *dep.*	to go out
egredior egredi egressus sum	
item *adv.*	likewise, also
agitare	to agitate
quamquam *conj.*	although

Unit 44

instruere instruo instruere instruxi instructum	to construct, instruct, organize
quotiens *adv.*	how often, so many
laedere laedo laedere laesi laesum	to hurt, harm, offend
pietas *f.*	piety, sense of duty
ruere ruo ruere rui rutum	to rush
singularis *adj.*	single, individual, singular
creber *adj.*	crowded, dense, numerous
immortalis *adj.*	immortal, everlasting
pretium *n.*	price, value, worth
curia *f.*	the curia (meeting house of the senate)
nimis *adv.*	too much, excessively
offendere offendo offendere offendi offensum	to offend, harm
permittere permitto permittere permisi permissum	to yield, permit, let go
perspicere perspicio perspicere perspexi perspectum	to examine, see into
condemnare	to condemn, sentence
proponere propono proponere proposui propositum	to propose, set out
ignarus *adj.*	ignorant, unknown
seditio *f.*	dissension, revolt
senator *m.*	senator
consentire consentio consentire consensi consensum	to agree, consent

Unit 45

iniquus *adj.*	uneven, unfair, unequal
undique *adv.*	on all sides
tristis *adj.*	sad
tectum *n.*	roof
flagitium *n.*	disgrace, shame
discrimen *n.*	division, crisis
donum *n.*	gift, present
ignorare	to be ignorant of
negligere	to neglect
negligo negligere neglexi neglectum	
ambo *num.*	both
portare	to carry, transport
brevis *adj.*	short, brief
quiescere	to rest, sleep
quiesco quiescere quievi quietum	
decimus *adj.*	tenth
umbra *f.*	shade, shadow
rarus *adj.*	scattered, rare
nuper *adv.*	recently
aequare	to make level, equalise
educere	to lead out, raise
educo educere eduxi eductum	
ecce *adv.*	look!

Unit 46

tellus *f.*	earth, land
altitudo *f.*	height
vestigium *n.*	footprint, trace
excitare	to awaken, raise up
insequi *dep.*	to follow after, pursue
insequor insequi	
insecutus sum	
natio *f.*	birth, nation, people
properare	to rush, hurry
desiderare	to desire, long for
claudere	to close
claudo claudere clausi	
clausum	
cupidus *adj.*	desiring, lusting
otium *n.*	leisure, idleness
parere	to give birth, produce
pario parere peperi	
partum	
stultus *adj.*	foolish, stupid
conservare	to preserve, keep, maintain
oppugnare	to attack, assault
herba *f.*	grass, herb
removere	to remove
removeo removere removi	
remotum	
restare	to remain, resist
resto restare restiti	
amnis *m.*	river, stream
efferre	to bring out, raise
effero efferre extuli	
elatum	

Unit 47

militia *f.*	active service, military
flrmus *adj.*	strong
varius *adj.*	various, varied
nuntius *m.*	messenger

prodere
    prodo prodere prodidi
    proditum
	to show, bring out, betray

commemorare	to recollect, remind
mirus *adj.*	wonderful, extraordinary

conspicere
    conspicio conspicere
    conspexi conspectum
	to see, perceive

labi *dep.* labor labi lapsus sum	to glide, slip
liberi *m. pl.*	children

terrere
    terreo terrere terrui
    territum
	to frighten, terrify

reprehendere
    reprehendo reprehendere
    reprehendi reprehensum
	to catch, blame

semel *adv.*	once
gradus *m.*	step

oblivisci *dep.*
    obliviscor oblivisci
    oblitus sum
	to forget

lucus *m.*	grove, wood
praeclarus *adj.*	brilliant, outstanding
ripa *f.*	shore, riverbank
universus *adj.*	entire, whole

occurrere
    occurro occurrere occurri
    occursum
	to run up to, happen

Unit 48

commodus *adj.*	proper, convenient, pleasant
triumphus *m.*	triumph
carere	to be lacking in, be without
careo carere carui	
deicere	to throw down, eject
deicio deicere deieci deiectum	
pondus *n.*	weight, importance
orator *m.*	speaker, orator
pergere	to continue, proceed with
pergo pergere perrexi perrectum	
praeesse	to be before, lead, command
praesum praeesse praefui	
magister *m.*	master, teacher
currus *m.*	chariot
haerere	to stick to, hang on to
haereo haerere haesi haesum	
origo *f.*	origin, source
finire	to finish, limit
respicere	to look back
respicio respicere respexi respectum	
differre	to scatter, spread about, differ
differo differre distuli dilatum	
frequens *adj.*	crowded, frequent
persequi *dep.*	to follow up, pursue, persecute
persequor persequi persecutus sum	
praecipere	to anticipate, instruct
pracipio praecipere praecepi praeceptum	
incertus *adj.*	uncertain, unsure
egere	to lack, want, need
egeo egere egui	

Unit 49

ingredi *dep.* ingredior ingredi ingressus sum	to enter
experiri *dep.* experior experiri expertus sum	to try, experience, test
flere fleo flere flevi fletum	to weep, cry
praeficere praeficio praeficere praefeci praefectum	to put in charge
infelix *adj.*	unhappy, unlucky, unfortunate
qualis *pron., adj.*	o f what kind, o f such a kind
nescius *adj.*	ignorant, unaware
levare	to lift up, lighten, relieve
animadvertere animadverto animadvertere animadverti animadversum	to notice, perceive
arcere arceo arcere arcui arcitum	to bow, arch
adversus *adj.*	towards, opposite, opposed
clamare	to shout, roar
augustus *adj.*	august, holy, majestic
discere disco discere didici	to learn
edicere edico edicere edixi edictum	to make known, proclaim
frui *dep.* fruor frui fructus (fruitus) sum	to enjoy, benefit from
furare	to rave, be mad
iuventus *f.*	youth
utinam *adv.*	if only, would that
ora *f.*	border, coast, limit

Unit 50

requirere
   requiro requirere
   requisii (requisivi) requisitum
	to seek, require, inquire

defensio *f.*	defence
fluctus *m.*	wave
difficilis *adj.*	difficult
num *part.*	it isn't, is it? (expecting 'no')
gloriari *dep.*	to boast of, glory in
manes *m. pl.*	ghosts, the Underworld
onus *n.*	burden
quaestor *m.*	quaestor
gaudium *n.*	joy
funus *n.*	funeral, corpse, death
suspicari *dep.*	to suspect
ultimus *adj.*	farthest
planus *adj.*	level, flat
facultas *f.*	faculty, power
notus *adj.*	known, distinguished, notorious
aptus *adj.*	joined, suitable, apt
celebrare	to crowd together, celebrate
firmare	to strengthen
durus *adj.*	hard, tough

Unit 51

serere	to plant, sow
sero serere sevi satum	
pudere	to be ashamed
pudeo pudere pudui	
puditum	
mortalis *adj.*	mortal
succedere	to advance, succeed
succedo succedere successi	
successum	
latus *adj.*	broad, wide
supra *adv., prep. + acc.*	above, over
tumultus *m.*	noise, uproar
mirari *dep.*	to wonder at, be astonished
impurus *adj.*	impure, unclean, shameful
conscribere	to enrol, write
conscribo conscribere	
conscripsi conscriptum	
plurimus *adj.*	most
emere	to buy, purchase
emo emere emi emptum	
idus *f. pl.*	the Ides (middle of Roman month)
odisse	to hate
odi odisse	
cursus *m.*	running, course
sponte *adv.*	spontaneously
arare	to plough
iucundus *adj.*	pleasant, agreeable
turba *f.*	mob, crowd
exprimere	to press, express
exprimo exprimere	
expressi expressum	

Unit 52

legatio f.	legation, embassy
tener adj.	tender, soft
pius adj.	pious, dutiful
morbus m.	sickness, disease
producere	to produce
produco producere produxi productum	
sedes f.	seat
inferus adj.	below
necare	to kill
tela f.	web
recusare	to refuse, reject
prodesse	to be of use, be advantageous
prosum prodesse profui	
reducere	to bring back, draw back,
reduco reducere reduxi reductum	reduce
abducere	to lead away
abduco abducere abduxi abductum	
conicere	to throw together
conicio conicere conieci conectum	
interficere	to kill
interficio interficere interfeci interfectum	
latus n.	side, flank
adiuvare	to help
adiuvo adiuvare adiuvi adiutum	
arguere	to prove, argue, accuse
arguo arguere argui argutum	
mensis m.	month
effundere	to pour out
effundo effundere effudi effusum	

Unit 53

spoliare	to strip, despoil
ornamentum *n.*	adornment, decoration
parcere	to spare, use sparingly
parco parcere peperci	
parsum	
florere	to flower, bloom, flourish
floreo florere florui	
quamvis *adv., conj.*	as much as you please, very much, although
nuptiae *f. pl.*	marriage, nuptials
sedare	to calm down, soothe
clades *f.*	disaster, destruction
convertere	to turn around, convert
converto convertere	
converti conversum	
forma *f.*	form, image
sin *conj.*	but if
ictus *m.*	blow, strike
incendium *n.*	fire
apparere	to appear
appareo apparere apparui	
apparitum	
vicis *adv.*	alternatively, in place o f
desinere	to cease, stop
desino desinere desii	
desitum	
ecquis *pron.*	whether any
providere	to see-ahead, provide for
provideo providere providi	
provisum	
simulare	to pretend, simulate
nepos *m.*	grandchild, nephew, descendant

Unit 54

confiteri *dep.*
   confiteor confiteri
   confessus sum
	to confess, admit

decedere
   decedo decedere decessi
   decessum
	to go away, yield, withdraw

subitus *adj.*	sudden, unexpected
ater *adj.*	black, dark

surgere
   surgo surgere surrexi
   surrectum
	to get up, grow up, raise up

decem *num.*	ten
vivus *adj.*	living, alive
vulnerare	to wound, injure
convivium *n.*	banquet, party
centum *num.*	hundred
incredibilis *adj.*	unbelievable, incredible
cornu *n.*	horn
calamitas *f.*	disaster
lepidus *adj.*	charming, nice
sinus *m.*	curve, bend

descendere
   descendo descendere
   descendi descensum
	to descend

eligere eligo eligere elegi electum	to choose, select
peccare	to make a mistake, commit a sin
hora *f.*	hour

incedere
   incedo incedere incessi
   incessum
	to go, happen

Unit 55

occasio *f.*	occasion, opportunity
leno *m.*	pimp
monumentum *n.*	memorial, monument
navare	to act energetically
adventus *m.*	arrival
omen *n.*	omen
decus *n.*	honour, glory

spargere
    spargo spargere sparsi
    sparsum
	to sprinkle, scatter

tardus *adj.*	slow, lazy, late
argumentum *n.*	argument
fames *f.*	hunger, famine

considere
    consido considere consedi
    consessum
	to sit down, stop

fraus *f.*	deception, fraud
insignis *adj.*	remarkable, eminent
vehemens *adj.*	furious, vehement

polliceri *dep.*
    polliceor polliceri
    pollicitus sum
	to promise

urgere urgeo urgere ursi	to urge, press upon
urbanus *adj.*	urban, urbane

admonere
    admoneo admonere
    admonui admonitum
	to remind, admonish

invidere
    invideo invidere invidi
    invisum
	to envy, be jealous of

Unit 56

obvius *adj.*	in the way, opposing
mala *f.*	cheek
suadere	to advise, persuade
suadeo suadere suasi	
suasum	
captare	to grasp at, seize, captivate
civilis *adj.*	relating to a Roman citizen, civil
nare	to swim
tribus *f.*	tribe
deponere	to place, put down
depono deponere	
deposui (deposivi)	
depositum	
designare	to mark out, arrange
demonstrare	to show, demonstrate
dulcis *adj.*	sweet
interdum *adv.*	sometimes, occasionally
pontus *n.*	sea
superbus *adj.*	proud, arrogant
adicere	to throw at, add
adicio adicere adieci	
adiectum	
adiungere	to add on, join
adiungo adiungere adiunxi	
adiunctum	
indicium *n.*	sign, evidence
flectere	to bend
flecto flectere flexi	
flexum	
incolumis *adj.*	unharmed, safe
municipium *n.*	township

Unit 57

potens *adj.*	powerful, capable
dolus	trick, deceit, fraud
resistere	to stop, resist
resisto resistere restiti	
vincire	to bind, tie up
vincio vincire vinxi	
vinctum	
superesse	to be above, survive
supersum superesse	
superfui	
egregius *adj.*	outstanding, excellent
rumor *m.*	noise, gossip, rumour
concurrere	to run together, concur
concurro concurrere	
concurri concursum	
interire	to die
intereo interire	
interii (interivi) interitum	
pingere	to paint, colour
pingo pingere pinxi pictum	
privatus *adj.*	private
rumpere	to break, smash
rumpo rumpere rupi ruptum	
invadere	to go in, attack, invade
invado invadere invasi	
invasum	
mora *f.*	delay, pause
contentio *f.*	dispute, contention
ter *adv.*	three times, thrice
navigare	to sail, navigate
venenum *n.*	poison, drug
contumelia *f.*	insult
corrumpere	to destroy, weaken, corrupt
corrumpo corrumpere	
corrupi corruptum	

Unit 58

hospitium *n.*	hospitality
deficere	to revolt, fail
deficio deficere defeci defectum	
delectare	to delight
manare	to drip, flow
humanitas *f.*	humanity, human nature
indulgere	to gratify, indulge in
indulgeo indulgere indulsi indulsum	
passus *m.*	step, pace, stride
lugere	to mourn, grieve
lugeo lugere luxi luctum	
robur *n.*	oak, strength
paternus *adj.*	fatherly
simulacrum *n.*	likeness, painting, statue
comes *c.*	companion, comrade, attendant
fessus *adj.*	tired, exhausted
minimus *adj.*	smallest
dimicare	to struggle, fight
nudus *adj.*	naked, bare
hiems *f.*	winter, storm
error *m.*	wandering, error, mistake
perpetuus *adj.*	continuous, perpetual
prudens *adj.*	prudent, clever, wise

Unit 59

tractare	to drag, pull
fluvius *m.*	river
hostilis *adj.*	hostile
audax *adj.*	bold, daring
dives *adj.*	rich, wealthy
innocens *adj.*	innocent, harmless
taurus *m.*	bull
intendere	to extend, direct, intend
intendo intendere intendi	
intentum	
liber *m.*	book
subsidium *n.*	aid, help
os *(gen.* ossis) *n.*	bone
persuadere	to persuade, convince
persuadeo persuadere	
persuasi persuasum	
solum *n.*	base, bottom, earth
orbis *m.*	circle, wheel
venia *f.*	indulgence, pardon
consumere	to consume, destroy
consumo consumere	
consumpsi consumptum	
terere	to rub
tero terere trivi tritum	
acerbus *adj.*	bitter
vates *m.*	seer, prophet
componere	to put together, arrange,
compono componere	compose
composui compositum	

Unit 60

inopia *f.*	poverty, need
recedere	to withdraw, recede
recedo recedere recessi	
recessum	
bracchium *n.*	arm
secundum *adv., prep. + acc.*	after, behind
spernere	to reject, spurn
sperno spernere sprevi	
spretum	
bos *c.*	ox, bull, cow
eximere	to take away, remove
eximo eximere exemi	
exemptum	
externus *adj.*	outside, foreign, strange
explicare	to unfold, explain
explico explicare	
explicavi (explicui)	
explicatum (explicitum)	
gravitas *f.*	weight, seriousness, gravity
cogitatio *f.*	thinking, reflection
penitus *adv.*	inwardly, internally, entirely
corripere	to seize, plunder
corripio corripere corripui	
correptum	
humanus *adj.*	human
erigere	to raise up, erect, excite
erigo erigere erexi	
erectum	
quot *adj.*	how many, so many
spectaculum *n.*	show, spectacle
turris *f.*	tower
avus *m.*	grandfather
apertus *adj.*	open

Unit 61

ferox *adj.*	warlike , wild
colligere	to collect
colligo colligere collegi	
collectum	
expellere	to drive out, expel
expello expellere expuli	
expulsum	
crudelitas *f.*	cruelty
foedare	to pollute , spoil, dishonour
impellere	to strike against, impel
impello impellere impuli	
impulsum	
bibere	to drink
bibo bibere bibi bibitum	
silentium *n.*	silence
abicere	to throw away, throw down
abicio abicere abieci	
abiectum	
infestus *adj.*	hostile, aggressive
lacus *m.*	lake
ordiri *dep.*	to begin
ordior ordiri orsus sum	
humus *f.*	earth, ground , soil
ridere	to laugh , smile at
rideo ridere risi risum	
digitus *m.*	finger
harena *f.*	sand, beach
quaestio *f.*	seeking, inquiry
obicere	to throw in the way of, oppose
obicio obicere obieci	
obiectum	
observare	to watch, observe
aedificium *n.*	building

Unit 62

torquere	to twist, torture
torqueo torquere torsi tortum	
furtum *n.*	theft
viginti *num.*	twenty
interrogare	to question, interrogate
pendere	to weigh, consider
pendo pendere pependi pensum	
possessio *f.*	possession
silere	to be silent
sileo silere silui	
vinum *n.*	wine
necessitudo *f.*	necessity, bond, relationship
tutus *adj.*	safe
color *m.*	colour
domesticus *adj.*	domestic
paries *m.*	wall
limen *n.*	threshold
mentiri *dep.*	to lie
servitus *f.*	slavery, servitude
ulcisci *dep.*	to avenge
ulciscor ulcisci ultus sum	
utilitas *f.*	usefulness
attingere	to touch, attack
attingo attingere attigi attactum	
collum *n.*	neck

Unit 63

ultro *adv.*	furthermore, besides
ensis *m.*	sword
horrere	to bristle, shudder
horreo horrere	
horrui horritum	
membrum *n.*	limb, member, part
praetermittere	to let pass, omit
praetermitto praetermittere	
praetermisi praetermissum	
regina *f.*	queen
laetitia *f.*	joy, happiness
diligens *adj.*	diligent, careful
sensus *m.*	feeling, perception
merces *f.*	pay, wages, interest
statua *f.*	statue
captus *m.*	seizing, taking
dudum *adv.*	not long ago
clam *adv.*	silently, secretly
continuus *adj.*	continuous, unbroken
emittere	to send out, dispatch, release
emitto emittere	
emisi emissum	
ramus *m.*	branch
heres *c.*	heir
nubere	to marry
nubo nubere	
nupsi nuptum	
obstare	to oppose, hinder
obsto obstare obstiti	

Unit 64

visum *n.*	vision
sextus *adj.*	sixth
favere	to favour, be devoted to
faveo favere favi fautum	
prae *adv., prep. + abl.*	before, because of
incendere	to burn
incendo incendere incendi	
incensum	
custodia *f.*	custody, protection
lavare	to wash, bathe
quies *f.*	rest, quiet
temere *adv.*	rashly
celare	to hide, conceal
undare	to rise in waves, surge
atrox *adj.*	terrible, cruel
consistere	to take a stand, remain
consisto consistere	
constiti constitum	
timidus *adj.*	fearful, timid
munitio *f.*	fortifying
corona *f.*	crown, wreath
crescere	to grow, swell
cresco crescere	
crevi cretum	
implere	to fill up, fulfil
impleo implere	
implevi impletum	
ferire	to strike, hit
vehere	to carry, transport
veho vehere vexi vectum	

Unit 65

germanus *adj.*	having the same parents
abstinere	to hold back, keep away from
abstineo abstinere	
abstinui abstentum	
concitare	to arouse, incite
aura *f.*	air, breeze
gignare	to create, bring forth
gigno gignare genui	
genitum	
includere	to enclose, blockade,
includo includere inclusi	
inclusum	
concordia *f.*	agreement, peace, harmony
aeger *adj.*	sick, ill
augurium *n.*	augury, prophecy
inanis *adj.*	empty, inane, vacant
misericordia *f.*	pity, compassion
gladius *m.*	sword
nequiquam *adv.*	in vain
secernere	to separate
secerno secernere secrevi	
secretum	
asper *adj.*	rough, harsh
umerus *m.*	shoulder
pridem *adv.*	long ago
assiduus *adj.*	established, steady
violare	to be violent to, violate
aggredior *dep.*	to approach, go to, attack
aggredior aggredi	
aggressus sum	

Unit 66

cingere
cingo cingere cinxi cinctum

to surround

conscius *adj.*

having knowledge of, conscious

exilium *n.*

exile, banishment

dissimulare

to conceal, disguise

formare

to shape, fashion

amarus *adj.*

bitter, harsh

munire

to fortify

praecipuus *adj.*

peculiar, special

triumphare

to triumph, have a triumph

vastare

to lay waste, ravage

aestimare

to estimate

principium *n.*

origin, beginning, cause

annare

to swim up to

complecti *dep.*
complector complecti complexus sum

to embrace

evadere
evado evadere evasi evasum

to go out, evade

excedere
excedo excedere excessi excessum

to go away, exceed

spiritus *m.*

breathing, breath, spirit

fulmen *n.*

lightning, thunderbolt

insigne *n.*

medal, decoration

vertex *m.*

whirlpool, eddy

Unit 67

existimatio *f.*	reputation, estimation
virere	to be green, healthy
vireo virere virui viritum	
contrahere	to collect, contract, reduce
contraho contrahere	
contraxi contractum	
matrimonium *n.*	marriage
propinquus *adj.*	near, neighbouring
intra *adv., prep. + acc.*	within
consequi *dep.*	to follow, pursue
consequor consequi	
consecutus sum	
fremere	to groan, roar
fremo fremere fremui	
fremitum	
nusquam *adv.*	nowhere
idoneus *adj.*	suitable, appropriate
militaris *adj.*	military
nancisci *dep.*	to get, acquire
nanciscor nancisci	
nanctus sum	
vicinus *adj.*	neighbouring
motus *m.*	motion, movement
quaestus *m.*	profit, gain
decipere	to deceive, cheat
decipio decipere decepi	
deceptum	
senectus *f.*	old age
occulare	to cover, hide, conceal
statio *f.*	standing, station
septem *num.*	seven

Unit 68

pendere pendeo pendere pependi	to hang, hang down

affligere
    affligo affligere afflixi
    afflictum
	to beat, strike

castellum *n.*	castle, fort
invitare	to invite
explorare	to seek out, explore
severus *adj.*	severe, stern
maestus *adj.*	sad, grieving, sorrowful
passim *adv.*	here and there, indiscriminately
aether *m.*	air, sky, heaven

perscribere
    perscribo perscribere
    perscripsi perscriptum
	to write out in full, note

quoad *adv.*	how far
praecipitare	to send headlong, throw down

profiteri   *dep.*
    profiteor profiteri
    professus sum
	to promise, confess

durare	to harden

sternere
    sterno sternere stravi
    stratum
	to spread out

immanis *adj.*	huge, monstrous
versus *adv., prep. + acc.*	towards

amplecti   *dep.*
    amplector amplecti
    amplexus sum
	to embrace

avaritia *f.*	avarice
densus *adj.*	thick, dense

Unit 69

vindicare	to claim, avenge
eicere	to throw out, expel, eject
eicio eicere eieci eiectum	
haurire	to drain
haurio haurire hausi haustum	
peragere	to finish, end
perago peragere peregi peractum	
maritus *m.*	husband
suspendere	to hang, suspend
suspendo suspendere suspendi suspensum	
cessare	to cease, be idle
adversarius *adj.*	turned towards, opposed
fretus *adj.*	relying on
aestas *f.*	summer
comere	to arrange
como comere compsi comptum	
discordia *f.*	disagreement, dissension
parum *adv.*	too little, insufficient
idcirco *adv.*	for that reason, on account o f
super *adv prep* + *acc & abl.*	above, beyond, in addition to
metiri *dep.*	to measure, estimate
metior metiri mensus sum	
minuere	to lessen, diminish
minuo minuere minui minutum	
nocturnus *adj.*	nocturnal
felix *adj.*	lucky, fortunate
obire	to go to, meet, die
obeo obire obii (obivi) obitum	

Unit 70

spatiari *dep.*	to walk about
supplex *adj.*	suppliant
gravare	to burden, load
testamentum *n.*	will, testament
villa *f.*	villa, estate
celer *adj.*	quick
theatrum *n.*	theatre
cibus *m.*	food
ingratus *adj.*	thankless, ungrateful
crinis *m.*	hair
delere	to destroy
deleo delere delevi	
deletum	
exitium *n.*	destruction, ruin
illustris *adj.*	bright, illustrious
desiderium *n.*	desire
septimus *adj.*	seventh
remus *m.*	oar
gestare	to carry, bear, wear
comperire	to find out, discover
comperio comperire	
comperi comperitum	
declarare	to declare, explain
ignominia *f.*	loss of reputation, disgrace

Unit 71

celeritas *f.*	speed
pascere	to nourish, feed
pasco pascere pavi pastum	
diligentia *f.*	diligence, carefulness
praemittere	to send ahead
praemitto praemittere	
praemisi praemissum	
saevire	to act savagely, rage
saevio saevire saevii	
saevitum	
ubique *adv.*	everywhere
caro *f.*	meat, flesh
velare	to cover, conceal
arbitrium *n.*	decision, choice
properus *adj.*	quick, hasty
patricius *adj.*	noble, patrician
coire	to come together, assemble
coeo coire coii (coivi)	
coitum	
propterea *adv.*	therefore
expetere	to desire, seek out
expeto expetere	
expetii (expetivi) expetitum	
hortari *dep.*	to encourage, urge on, incite
interimere	to kill, destroy
interimo interimere	
interemi interemptum	
nemus *n.*	wood, forest
capillus *m.*	hair
rescribere	rewrite, write back
rescribo rescribere rescripsi	
rescriptum	
severitas *f.*	severity, sternness

Unit 72

admittere
    admitto admittere admisi
    admissum
to send to, permit, admit

sufferare — to support, suffer

vacare — to be empty, be free from

meritum   *n.* — punishment, reward

barbarus   *adj.* — foreign, barbarian

complere — to fill up, complete
    compleo complere
    complevi completum

demittere — to send down, drop
    demitto demittere
    demisi demissum

exitus   *m.* — departure, exit, end

cervix   *f.* — neck

fidelis   *adj.* — faithful, loyal

inimicitia   *f.* — enmity, hostility

lapis   *m.* — stone

collis   *m.* — hill

monstrare — to show, reveal

potiri   *dep.* — to get power over, acquire

aeternus   *adj.* — eternal

securus   *adj.* — secure, unconcerned

sufficere — to suffuse, supply, suffice
    sufficio sufficere
    suffeci suffectum

virga   *f.* — twig, stick

vigilare — to be awake, be on watch

Unit 73

paulatim *adv.*	little by little, gradually
avidus *adj.*	greedy, keen
cito *adv.*	quickly
imber *m.*	rain, storm
sollicitare	to disturb, harass, agitate
compellere	to drive, coerce
compello compellere	
compuli compulsum	
divinus *adj.*	divine, godlike
fundus *m.*	base, foundation, farm
increpare	to rattle
increpo increpare	
increpavi (increpui)	
increpatum (increpitum)	
praetorius *adj.*	praetorian
insuper *adv.*	above, overhead
miseria *f.*	wretchedness, misery
percutere	to hit, strike
percutio percutere	
percussi percussum	
prospicere	to look ahead, anticipate, foresee
perspicio perspicere	
perspexi perspectum	
censor *m.*	the censor
saltus *m.*	jump, leap, pasture, ravine
aevum *n.*	age, eternity
effugere	to flee
effugio effugere effugi	
effugitum	
avis *f.*	bird
decretum *n.*	decision, decree

Unit 74

contrarius *adj.*	opposite, contrary, hostile
eloqui *dep.*	to speak out, express
eloquor eloqui elocutus sum	
vexare	to annoy, vex
excludere	to shut out, exclude
excludo excludere exclusi	
exclusum	
gemere	to groan, sigh
gemo gemere gemui	
gemitum	
inesse	to be in
insum inesse infui	
pestis *f.*	plague, disaster
posthac *adv.*	after this, hereafter
nefas *n.*	evil, sin
incitare	to spur on, incite
puppis *f.*	stern of a ship
veteranus *adj.*	veteran
vetustas *f.*	age, antiquity
administrare	to help
festinare	to hurry, rush
circus *m.*	circle, circus
struere	to arrange, build
struo struere struxi	
structum	
claudus *adj.*	limping, lame
dens *m.*	tooth
honestum *n.*	morality, virtue, beauty

Unit 75

infimus *adj.*	lowest
praeceps *adj.*	headlong
arcus *m.*	bow, arch
geminus *adj.*	twin
natare	to swim
praedo *m.*	robber
velum *n.*	cloth, curtain
ala *f.*	wing
captivus *m.*	captive, prisoner
coercere	to confine, restrain
coerceo coercere coercui coercitum	
neve, neu *adv.*	and not, nor
coniunctio *f.*	joining together, marriage
dignare	to consider worthy
valetudo *f.*	health
grandis *adj.*	great, large
intercedere	to go between, intervene
intercedo intercedere intercessi intercessum	
materia *f.*	material, matter
coniuratio *f.*	union, conspiracy
nempe *conj.*	indeed, to be sure, truly
onerare	to load, burden

Unit 76

sagitta *f.*	arrow
praeferre	to carry before, prefer
praefero praeferre praetuli praelatum	
prosequi *dep.*	to accompany, follow
prosequor prosequi prosecutus sum	
saeculum *n.*	generation, lifetime, era, century
trepidus *adj.*	fearful, agitated
agnoscere	to recognise, acknowledge
agnosco agnoscere agnovi agnitum	
placidus *adj.*	agreeable, pleasant
communire	to fortify
communio communire communii (communivi) communitum	
considerare	to consider, contemplate
frustra *adv.*	in vain
ratis *f.*	raft
gladiator *m.*	gladiator
proinde *adv.*	just as, therefore
carpere	to pluck, seize
carpo carpere carpsi carptum	
repellere	to drive back, repel
repello repellere repuli repulsum	
sacrificium *n.*	sacrifice
protinus *adv.*	immediately
commeatus *m.*	trade, commerce
stirps *f.*	stalk, stem
agrestis *adj.*	rural, rustic

Unit 77

habitus *m.*	condition, appearance
profecto *adv.*	certainly, truly, indeed
complures *adj.*	very many
duplex *adj.*	double, two-fold
nefarius *adj.*	impious
excusare	to excuse
cupido *f.*	desire, greed
expugnare	to capture, subdue
formido *f.*	fear
genitor *m.*	father
equitatus *m.*	cavalry, equestrian order
vulgare	to make well-known, publish
nudare	to bare, uncover, strip
obscurus *adj.*	obscure, dark
fodere	to dig
fodio fodere fodi fossum	
quartus *adj.*	fourth
tenuis *adj.*	thin, slender
circumvenire	to surround, cheat
circumvenio circumvenire	
circumveni circumventum	
sepulcrum *n.*	grave, sepulchre
desperare	to despair, give up

Unit 78

figura *f.*	form, shape
erumpere	to break out, burst out
erumpo erumpere erupi	
eruptum	
vacuus *adj.*	empty, free from
impudens *adj.*	shameless, impudent
favor *m.*	favour, goodwill
ostium *n.*	doorway, entrance
potentia *f.*	power, force
subvenire	to support, aid
subvenio subvenire subveni	
subventum	
fructus *m.*	enjoyment, profit
immensus *adj.*	vast, immense
tumulus *m.*	mound
aestus *m.*	heat
circumdare	to surround, encircle
circumdo circumdare	
circumdedi circumdatum	
constantia *f.*	firmness, perseverance
destinare	to determine, intend
negotiari *dep.*	to trade, be in business
purgare	to clean, purge
dirus *adj.*	horrible, dire
excutere	to shake off
excutio excutere excussi	
excussum	
fluere	to flow
fluo fluere fluxi fluxum	

Unit 79

urere uro urere ussi ustum	to burn
imus *adj.*	lowest
lectus *m.*	bed ,couch
colonus *m.*	farmer, colonist
illico *adv.*	in that very place, immediately
precari *dep.*	to beg, pray
socer *m.*	father-in-law

accendere
   accendo accendere accendi
   accensum
	to set on fire

usquam *adv.*	anywhere

depellere
   depello depellere depuli
   depulsum
	to drive off, expel

subigere
   subigo subigere subegi
   subactum
	to drive under, subject

tametsi *conj.*	nevertheless, although
extra *adv., prep.* + *acc.*	outside, beyond
verberare	to beat, hit

interponere
   interpono interponere
   interposui interpositum
	to place between, interpose

visus *m.*	sight
studiosus *adj.*	eager, zealous
perturbare	to confuse, upset
impedimentum *n.*	obstacle, hindrance, baggage
segnis *adj.*	slow, sluggish

Unit 80

benevolentia *f.*	goodwill, benevolence
patruus *m.*	uncle
aliquot *num.*	several, some
redigere	to drive back, reduce
redigo redigere redegi redactum	
nobilitas *f.*	nobility, fame
mitis *adj.*	mild, gentle, ripe
crassus *adj.*	thick, fat, crass
aequitas *f.*	evenness, fairness
sapientia *f.*	wisdom
opponere	to place opposite, oppose
oppono opponere opposui oppositum	
perducere	to bring over, persuade
perduco perducere perduxi perductum	
induere	to put on, clothe
induo induere indui indutum	
spolium *n.*	booty, spoils
nauta *m.*	sailor
astare	to stand by
asto astare astiti	
consultum *n.*	decree, decision
lucere	to shine
luceo lucere luxi	
minae *f. pl.*	battlements, threats
pertimescere	to be very afraid
pertimesco pertimescere pertimui	
repentinus *adj.*	sudden, unexpected

Unit 81

ultra *adv., prep. + acc.*	beyond
admovere	to move, bring to
admoveo admovere admovi	
admotum	
rostrum *n.*	beak, prow, speaker's platform
tabella *f*	board, tray, writing tablet
ardor *m.*	burning, heat, eagerness
cruor *m.*	blood, bloodshed
disponere	to place, arrange, distribute
dispono disponere disposui	
dispositum	
tyrannus *m.*	tyrant
minari *dep.*	to threaten, menace
similitudo *f.*	likeness, resemblance
evertere	to overturn, overthrow
everto evertere everti	
eversum	
fovere	to keep warm, foster
foveo fovere fovi fotum	
scutum *n.*	shield
moles *f.*	mass, heap
patefacere	to reveal
patefacio patefecere	
patefeci patefactum	
concilium *n.*	assembly, council
secare	to cut
seco secare secui sectum	
pavor *m.*	fear, trembling
sollicitus *adj.*	worried, agitated
mollis *adj.*	soft, gentle

Unit 82

religiosus *adj.*	religious, reverent, superstitious
operire	to cover, hide
operio operire operui	
opertum	
custodire	to guard
ruina *f.*	collapse, ruin, destruction
lacrimare	to cry
longitudo *f.*	length
pridie *adv.*	on the day before yesterday
pariter *adv.*	alike, likewise, at the same time
inclinare	to bend, influence
studere	to be eager
studeo studere studui	
flagitare	to demand, entreat
totidem *num.*	just as many
disputare	to discuss, argue
trepidare	to be fearful, tremble
aditus *m.*	approach, access
pronuntiare	to pronounce
aedificare	to build
traducere	to lead over, bring across
traduco traducere traduxi	
traductum	
commendatio *f.*	recommendation, commendation
denuntiare	to denounce

Unit 83

monstrum *n.*	omen, monster
eheu *interj.*	alas! oh no!
luna *f.*	moon
lacessere	to provoke, irritate
lacesso lacessere lacessivi lacessitum	
mandatum *n.*	order, commission
valles *f.*	valley
neuter *adj.*	neither of two
prodire	to go, appear
prodeo prodire prodii proditum	
luctus *m.*	mourning, grief
querela *f.*	complaint
renuntiare	to report, renounce
lupus *m.*	wolf
reservare	to reserve, conserve
inops *adj.*	lacking, poor
splendor *m.*	brightness, splendour
usurpare	to seize, usurp
admirari *dep.*	to admire
exspectatio *f.*	waiting for, expectation
satis *adv., adj.*	enough, sufficient
insanus *adj.*	insane

Unit 84

maternus *adj.*	maternal
petitio *f.*	attack, petition, request
elicere	to allure, entice out, elicit
elicio elicere elicui elictum	
caelestis *adj.*	celestial, heavenly
porticus *f.*	gate
fatigare	to tire, wear out
progredi *dep.*	to progress, proceed
progredior progredi	
progressus sum	
sepelire	to bury
sepelio sepelire	
sepelii (sepelivi) sepultum	
dedicare	to declare, dedicate
temeritas *f.*	rashness
venus *f.*	charm, loveliness
carcer *m.*	jail, prison
toga *f.*	toga
dissolvere	to loosen, dissolve, destroy
dissolvo dissolvere dissolvi	
dissolutum	
praefectus *m.*	prefect
en *interj.*	look!
evocare	to call out, summon
praedium *n.*	estate
fungi *dep.*	to perform, occupy oneself
fungor fungi functus sum	
imminere	to overhang, threaten
immineo imminere imminui	

Unit 85

benignus *adj.*	kindly, generous, liberal
iners *adj.*	unskilled, lazy
pulsare	to hit, beat
iuventa *f.*	youth
deprehendere	to catch, seize
deprehendo deprehendere	
deprehendi deprehensum	
licentia *f.*	licence
minister *m.*	attendant, servant
cor *n.*	heart
deditio *f.*	surrender, capitulation
partus *m.*	birth, offspring
amens *adj.*	mad, insane
penna *f.*	feather
proles *f.*	progeny, offspring, descendants
institutum *n.*	undertaking, institution
recordari *dep.*	to remember, recollect
saltem *adv.*	at least
infensus *adj.*	hostile, angry
secundo *adv.*	secondly
vilis *adj.*	cheap, worthless
impius *adj.*	impious, godless

Unit 86

praeponere
    praepono praeponere
    praeposui praepositum
	to place before, prefer

triginta *num.*	thirty
aptare	to adapt to, prepare
familiaritas *f.*	friendship, familiarity
lignum *n.*	wood
colloquium *n.*	talk, conversation
manifestus *adj.*	clear, evident, manifest
postridie *adv.*	on the following day
purpureus *adj.*	purple

describere
    describo describere
    descripsi descriptum
	to describe

saevitia *f.*	ferocity
umbrare	to overshadow
varietas *f.*	variety
canis *c.*	dog
ferreus *adj.*	made of iron
cantare	to sing, play
cliens *m.*	client
uber *n., adj.*	udder, rich, fruitful
pelagus *n.*	sea, ocean
consecrare	to consecrate, deify

Unit 87

imperitus *adj.*	unskilled, inexperienced
permanere	to remain, last
permaneo permanere	
permansi permansum	
deprecari *dep.*	to pray
implorare	to implore
exuere	to take off
exuo exuere exuie exutum	
liberalitas *f.*	generosity, noble character
collegium *n.*	college, guild
obruere	to cover, overwhelm
obruo obruere obrui	
obrutum	
scelerare	to comm it a crime, pollute
tormentum *n.*	torture
admodum *adv.*	completely
coronare	to crown, surround
cinis *m.*	ashes
reicere	to throw back, reject
reicio reicere reieci	
reiectum	
liberalis *adj.*	honest, liberal
comparatio *f.*	comparison
dormire	to sleep
lentus *adj.*	slow
callidus *adj.*	clever, skilful
expers *adj.*	lacking

Unit 88

vetustus *adj.*	old, ancient
laevus *adj.*	left, stupid, unlucky
flagrare	to burn
secus *adv.*	otherwise
irritus *adj.*	invalid, void
lenire	to alleviate, mollify
piscis *m.*	fish
reditus *m.*	return
vigilia *f.*	nightwatch, vigilance
remanere	to remain
remaneo remanere remansi remansum	
veritas *f.*	truth
albus *adj.*	white
rogitare	to ask frequently
circum *adv., prep. + acc.*	around, about
stringere	to draw tight
stringo stringere strinxi strictum	
trans *prep. + acc.*	across, over
stipendium *n.*	pay, tax
perterrere	to terrify
perterreo perterrere perterrui perterritum	
unicus *adj.*	unique, sole
confugere	to flee
confugio confugere confugi	

Unit 89

periculosus *adj.*	dangerous, hazardous
congredi *dep.*	to meet, engage
congredior congredi	
congressus sum	
pernicies *f.*	destruction, danger
excellere	to excel
excello excellere excellui	
excelsum	
mediocris *adj.*	ordinary, mediocre
exhaurire	to drain, exhaust
exhaurio exhaurire exhausi	
exhaustum	
fere, ferme *adv.*	almost
reliquiae *f. pl.*	relics, remains
oraculum *n.*	oracle, prophecy
pristinus *adj.*	former, previous
coram *adv.*	face to face
solacium *n.*	comfort, consolation
transigere	to stab, finish
transigo transigere transegi	
transactum	
vadere	to go, rush
vado vadere vasi vasum	
cella *f.*	storeroom
vena *f.*	vein
agricola *m.*	farmer
nympha *f.*	nymph, newly-wed
exstinguere	to extinguish
exstinguo exstinguere	
exstinxi exstinctum	
frumentarius *adj.*	relating to the grain supply

Unit 90

hereditas *f.*	inheritance
poculum *n.*	cup
gratulari *dep.*	to congratulate, rejoice
missus *m.*	sending, shooting
sonus *m.*	sound, noise
plaudere	to beat, strike, clap
plaudo plaudere plausi plausum	
ignotus *adj.*	unknown
linquere	to leave, relinquish
linquo linquere liqui lictum	
nota *f.*	mark, note
iracundia *f.*	anger
librare	to keep in balance, brandish
palam *adv.*	openly, explicitly
confundere	to pour together, confuse
confundo confundere confudi confusum	
rogus *m.*	funeral pile
vestire	to clothe
vestio vestire vestii (vestivi) vestitum	
deterrere	to deter, discourage
deterreo deterrere deterrui deterritum	
auxiliari *dep.*	to help
vallum *n.*	fortification
cavus *adj.*	hollow
conducere	to collect, bring together
conduco conducere conduxi conductum	

Unit 91

leo *m.*	lion
epulae *f. pl.*	banquet, feast
insidiari *dep.*	to am bush
novem *num.*	nine
augur *c.*	seer, augur, soothsayer
lucrum *n.*	gain, profit
persona *f.*	role, personality
demere	to remove
demo demere dempsi	
demptum	
stuprum *n.*	debauchery, violation
advocare	to summon, call
largitio *f.*	largesse
cognomen *n.*	family name, surname
fas *n.*	divine law
finitimus *adj.*	neighbouring
industrius *adj.*	active, industrious
defensor *m.*	defender, protector
fastigium *n.*	summit
ianua *f.*	door, doorway
partire	to divide, share
irrumpere	to burst in
irrumpo irrumpere irrupi	
irruptum	

Unit 92

oppido *adv.* — very much, greatly

antrum *n.* — cave, den

peregrinus *adj.* — foreign, strange

ortus *m.* — birth, rising

percellere — to hit, knock, strike
  percello percellere perculi perculsum

rogatio *f.* — asking, question

possidere — to possess
  possideo possidere possedi possessum

perfidia *f.* — treachery

falsus *adj.* — false

stella *f.* — star

securis *f.* — axe

sistere — to stand, place
  sisto sistere stiti statum

obsidio *f.* — siege, blockade

maturus *adj.* — ripe, mature

praesentire — to feel beforehand
  praesentio praesentire praesensi praesensum

beatus *adj.* — happy, blessed

fulgere — to shine
  fulgeo fulgere fulsi

lenis *adj.* — mild, gentle, soft

pulvis *m.* — dust

partiri *dep.* — to divide, share

Unit 93

superbia *f.*	pride, arrogance
inermis *adj.*	unarmed
commutare	to change, alter
aequalis *adj.*	equal, flat, level
sinister *adj.*	left, wrong, unlucky
rapidus *adj.*	swift, quick
trabs *f.*	tree-trunk, beam
meditari *dep.*	to think, prepare to
attollere	to raise up, lift up
attollo attollere	
circa *adv., prep. + acc.*	about, around
adipisci *dep.*	to acquire, obtain
adipiscor adipisci	
adeptus sum	
comprehendere	to grasp, comprehend
comprehendo comprehendere	
comprehendi comprehensum	
fatalis *adj.*	fated, fatal
exiguus *adj.*	small, little
cotidie *adv.*	daily
rota *f.*	wheel
flare	to blow
coitus *m.*	coming together, union, connection
irridere	to laugh at, ridicule
irrideo irridere irrisi	
irrisum	
ornatus *adj.*	adorned, decorated

tremere tremo tremere tremui	to tremble
pastor *m.*	shepherd
vicus *m.*	village, district
canere caneo canere canui	to be white
rusticus *adj.*	rustic, rural
scaena *f.*	stage

defungi   *dep.*
   defungor defungi
   defunctus sum
	to finish, complete

trucidare	to slaughter
scientia *f.*	knowledge
comitari *dep.*	to accompany
servitium *n.*	servitude, slavery
solitudo *f.*	solitude, loneliness

comprimere
   comprimo comprimere
   compressi compressum
	to compress, restrain, crush

sodalis *m.*	comrade

apponere
   appono apponere apposui
   appositum
	to place near, appoint

adigere
   adigo adigere adegi
   adactum
	to drive to, compel

circumire
   circumeo (circueo) circumire
   circumii (circumivi) circuitum
	to go around

virilis *adj.*	male, manly, virile
serus *adj.*	late, too late
deterior *adj.*	worse

Unit 95

flavus *adj.* — golden, yellow,

pavidus *adj.* — scared, frightened

eniti *dep.* — to struggle, strive
  enitor eniti
  enisus (enixus) sum

frequentare — to crowd together, frequent

agger *m.* — mound, rampart

comprobare — to approve, confirm

letum *n.* — death

capessere — to grasp, seize
  capesso capessere
  capessii (capessivi)
  capessitum

libellus *m.* — booklet

praesentia *f.* — presence

tutor *m.* — guardian

generare — to sire, create

anguis *c.* — snake

grex *m.* — herd, flock

confestim *adv.* — immediately

fiducia *f.* — trust

dedecus *n.* — shame, disgrace, dishonour

eximius *adj.* — exceptional, distinguished

cognatus *adj.* — related

fretum *n.* — strait, channel

Unit 96

maeror *m.*	mourning, grief
vastus *adj.*	empty, devastated
opperiri *dep.*	to wait, expect
opperior opperiri	
oppertus (opperitus) sum	
priscus *adj.*	ancient, antique
significatio *f.*	sign, indication
sordidus *adj.*	dirty, sordid
niger *adj.*	black
abnuere	to refuse, deny
abnuo abnuere abnui	
turpitudo *f.*	disgrace, turpitude
vanus *adj.*	empty, meaningless, vain
machina *f.*	device, machine
venerari *dep.*	to venerate
defectio *f.*	defection, rebellion
mollire	to soften, soothe
adolescere	to grow up
adolesco adolescere adolevi	
communicare	to communicate, inform, share
difficultas *f.*	difficulty
turma *f.*	troop, platoon
focus *m.*	hearth, fireplace
laetari *dep.*	to be joyful, be happy

Unit 97

praeditus *adj.*	endowed with
palma *f.*	hand, palm
nubes *f.*	cloud
obesse	to be in the way, hinder
obsum obesse obfui	
caecus *adj.*	blind
pauper *adj.*	poor
imitari *dep.*	to imitate
heus *interj.*	hi! hey!
pronus *adj.*	prone, stooping
adoriri *dep.*	to rise up, attack
adorior adoriri adortus sum	
caritas *f.*	dearness, affection
dictitare	to say often, reiterate
funis *m.*	rope, line
horridus *adj.*	rough, shaggy, trembling
opportunus *adj.*	suitable, appropriate, opportune
exoriri *dep.*	to rise up, proceed
exorior exoriri exortus sum	
ignavus *adj.*	lazy, idle
penetrare	to go into, penetrate
incumbere	to lie down on, rest on
incumbo incumbere	
incubui incubitum	
minor *adj.*	smaller

Unit 98

submittere	to place under, submit
submitto submittere	
submisi submissum	
octo *num.*	eight
collocare	to establish, place
profugere	to flee, escape
profugio profugere profugi	
eventus *m.*	event, outcome, result
radius *m.*	spoke of a wheel, stick
latro *m.*	robber, highwayman
popularis *adj.*	public, popular
vagus *adj.*	wandering, roaming
absumere	to take away, destroy
absumo absumere	
absumpsi absumptum	
adulterium *n.*	adultery
responsum *n.*	answer
concipere	to hold, conceive, commit
concipio concipere	
concepi conceptum	
infinitus *adj.*	infinite, endless
explere	to fill up, fulfil
expleo explere explevi	
expletum	
festus *adj.*	sacred, festive
sapiens *adj.*	wise
demum *adv.*	finally
latrocinium *n.*	robbery
modestus *adj.*	modest, restrained

Unit 99

assuescere	
assuesco assuescere	to grow accustomed to
assuevi assuetum	
cultus *m., adj.*	
murmur *n.*	cultivation, cultivated
privatim *adv.*	murmur
axis *m.*	privately
repudiare	axis, north pole
exsequi *dep.*	to refuse, reject
exsequor exsequi	to follow, accomplish
exsecutus sum	
retro *adv.*	backwards, behind
octavus *adj.*	eighth
sustentare	to support, sustain
porrigere	to reach out, stretch, hold out
porrigo porrigere porrexi	
porrectum	
tolerare	to endure, tolerate, support
videlicet *adv.*	clearly, namely
adimere	to take away
adimo adimere ademi	
ademptum	
arduus *adj.*	steep, difficult
concidere	fall, collapse, fail
concido concidere concidi	
tardare	to loiter, delay
conscientia *f.*	awareness, conscience
exquirere	to seek out
exquiro exquirere exquisivi	
exquisitum	
fauces *f. pl.*	jaws, mouth

Unit 100

nonus *adj.*	ninth
talentum *n.*	a talent (a weight of money)
paratus *adj.*	prepared, ready
victus *m.*	food, nourishment
peritus *adj.*	skilled in, expert

quatere
    quatio quatere quassi
    quassum
	to shake

simulatio *f.*	imitation, simulation
gelidus *adj.*	cold, icy
celeber *adj.*	famous
volumen *n.*	book, roll
folium *n.*	leaf
infamis *adj.*	infamous
radix *f.*	root
velox *adj.*	fast
invidiosus *adj.*	envious, hating
otiosus *adj.*	unoccupied, at leisure, idle
mundus *m.*	world, universe
anceps *adj.*	two-sided, undecided
diuturnus *adj.*	long-lasting
vitta *f.*	ribbon

Latin Index

a 1
ab 1
abducere 2
abesse 15
abicere 61
abire 13
abnuere 96
abstinere 65
absumere 98
ac 1
accedere 18
accendere 79
accidere 27
accipere 5
accusare 29
acer 28
acerbus 59
acies 22
ad 1
adducere 27
adeo 9
adesse 11
adhibere 40
adhuc 19
adicere 56
adigere 94
adimere 99
adipisci 93
aditus 82
adiungere 56
adiuvare 52
administrare 74
admiri 83
admittere 72
admodum 87
admonere 55
admovere 81
adolescere 96
adoriri 97
adulescens 29

adulterium 98
advenire 22
adventus 55
adversarius 69
adversus 49
advertere 32
advocare 91
aedere 37
aedes 19
aedificare 82
aedificium 61
aeger 65
aequalis 93
aequare 45
aequitas 80
aequor 41
aequus 27
aer 42
aestas 69
aestimare 66
aestus 78
aetas 13
aeternus 72
aether 68
aevum 73
afferre 14
afficere 39
affligere 68
ager 10
agere 3
agger 95
aggredi 65
agitare 43
agmen 21
agnoscere 76
agrestis 76
agricola 89
aiere 8
ala 75
albus 88

alere 19
alienus 31
aliquis 10
aliquot 80
aliter 35
alius 4
alter 8
altitudo 46
altus 37
amare 7
amarus 66
ambo 45
amens 85
amicitia 27
amicus 9
amittere 23
amnis 46
amor 11
amplecti 68
amplus 20
an 6
anceps 100
anguis 95
anima 29
animadvertere 49
animus 4
annare 66
annus 8
ante 5
antea 29
antiquus 31
antrum 92
aperire 27
apertus 60
apparere 53
appellere 13
apponere 94
apto 86
aptus 50
apud 5

aqua 14
ara 41
arare 51
arbitrium 71
arbor 35
arcere 49
arcus 75
ardere 33
ardor 81
arduus 99
argentum 24
arguere 52
argumentum 55
arma 11
armare 12
ars 32
artus 33
arx 42
asper 65
aspicere 32
assiduus 65
assuescere 99
astare 80
at 6
ater 54
atque 1
atrox 64
attingere 62
attollere 93
auctor 24
auctoritas 13
audacia 40
audax 59
audere 19
audire 6
auferre 25
augere 25
augur 91
augurium 65
augustus 49

aura 65
auris 28
aurum 13
auspicium 42
aut 2
autem 3
auxiliari 90
auxilium 35
avaritia 68
avertere 41
avidus 73
avis 73
avus 60
axis 99

barbarus 72
beatus 92
bellum 6
bene 15
beneficium 24
benevolentia 80
benignus 85
bibere 61
bis 42
bonus 5
bos 60
bracchium 60
brevis 45

cadere 17
caecus 97
caedere 23
caedes 29
caelestis 84
caelum 30
calamitas 54
callidus 87
campus 28
canere (caneo) 94
canere (cano) 42

canis 86
cantare 86
capere 8
capessere 95
capillus 71
captare 56
captivus 75
captus 63
caput 15
carcer 84
carere 48
caritas 97
carmen 35
caro 71
carpere 76
carus 41
castellum 68
castrum 17 ,
casus 36
causa 3
cavere 37
cavus 90
cedere 17
celare 64
celeber 100
celebrare 50
celer 70
celeritas 71
cella 89
censere 18
censor 73
centum 54
centurio 38
cernere 33
certamen 26
certare 33
certus 6
cervix 72
cessare 69
ceterus 17

cibus 70
cingere 66
cinis 87
circa 93
circum 88
circumdare 78
circumire 94
circumvenire 77
circus 74
cito 73
civilis 56
civis 9
civitas 6
clades 53
clam 63
clamare 49
clamor 29
clarus 21
classis 25
claudo 46
claudus 74
cliens 86
coepere 18
coercere 75
cogere 14
cogitare 21
cogitatio 60
cognatus 95
cognomen 91
cognoscere 10
cohors 25
coire 71
coitus 93
colere 22
collega 32
collegium 87
colligere 61
collis 72
collocare 98
colloquium 86

collum 62
colonia 42
colonus 79
color 62
comere 69
comes 58
comitari 94
comitium 38
commeatus 76
commemorare 47
commendare 38
commendatio 82
committere 27
commodus 48
commovere 39
communicare 96
communio 76
communis 35
commutare 93
comparare 23
comparatio 87
compellere 73
comperire 70
complecti 66
complere 72
complures 77
componere 59
comprehendere 93
comprimere 94
comprobare 95
conari 39
concedere 20
concidere 99
concilium 81
concipere 98
concitare 65
concordia 65
concurrere 57
condemnare 44
condere 39

condicio 31
conducere 90
conferre 23
confestim 95
conficere 40
confirmare 35
confiteri 54
confugere 88
confundere 90
congredi 89
conicere 52
coniunctio 75
coniungere 33
coniuratio 75
conscientia 99
conscius 66
conscribere 51
consecrare 86
consentire 44
consequi 67
conservare 46
considerare 76
considere 55
consilium 7
consistere 64
conspicere 47
constantia 78
constare 15
constituere 15
consuetudo 30
consul 6
consularis 38
consulatus 27
consulere 11
consultum 80
consumere 59 ,
contemnere 40
contendere 27
contentio 57
continere 27

contingere 41
continuus 63
contio 28
contra 8
contrahere 67
contrarius 74
contumelia 57
convenire 17
convertere 53
convivium 54
copia 14
cor 85
coram 89
cornu 54
corona 64
coronare 87
corpus 9
corripere 60
corrumpere 57
cotidie 93
crassus 80
creare 29
creber 44
credere 6
crescere 64
crimen 15
crinis 70
crudelis 41
crudelitas 61
cruor 81
culpa 43
cultus 99
cum 1
cunctus 29
cupere 18
cupiditas 36
cupido 77
cupidus 46
cur 13
cura 14

curare 12
curia 44
currere 28
currus 48
cursus 51
custodia 64
custodire 82
custos 42

damnare 35
dare 3
de 1
dea 34
debere 7
decedere 54
decem 54
decernere 21
decet 42
decimus 45
decipere 67
declarare 70
decretum 73
decus 55
dedecus 95
dedere 10
dedicare 84
deditio 85
deducere 30
deesse 21
defectio 96
defendere 12
defensio 50
defensor 91
deferre 22
deficere 58
defungor 94
deicere 48
deinde 9
delecto 58
delere 70

deligere 42
demere 91
demittere 72
demonstrare 56
demum 98
denique 17
dens 74
densus 68
denuntiare 82
depellere 79
deponere 56
deprecari 87
deprehendere 85
descendere 54
describere 86
deserere 36
desiderare 46
desiderium 70
designare 56
desinere 53
desperare 77
destinare 78
deterior 94
deterrere 90
deus 5
dexter 33
dicere 1
dictator 29
dictitare 97
dies 5
differre 48
difficilis 50
difficultas 96
digitus 61
dignare 75
dignitas 14
dignus 22
diligens 63
diligentia 71
diligere 23

dimicare 58
dimittere 31
dirus 78
discedere 24
discere 49
disciplina 43
discordia 69
discrimen 45
disponere 81
disputare 82
dissimulare 66
dissolvere 84
diu 16
diuturnus 100
dives 59
dividere 43
divinus 73
divus 19
docere 20
dolere 41
dolor 16
dolus 57
domare 38
domesticus 62
dominus 37
domus 5
donare 33
donec 36
donum 45
dormire 87
dubitare 19
dubius 33
ducere 19
dudum 63
dulcis 56
dum 7
duo 7
duplex 77
durare 68
durus 50

dux 14

e 2
ea 1
ecce 45
ecquis 53
edere 22
edicere 49
educere 45
efferre 46
efficere 23
effugere 73
effundere 52
egere 48
ego 1
egredi 43
egregius 57
eheu 83
eicere 69
elicere 84
eligere 54
eloqui 74
emere 51
emittere 63
en 84
enim 2
eniti 95
ensis 63
eodem 31
epistula 21
epulae 91
eques 17
equidem 25
equitatus 77
equus 17
erga 41
ergo 9
erigere 60
eripere 25
errare 36

error 58
erumpere 78
esse 1
et 1
etenim 38
etiam 2
etsi 23
evadere 66
evenire 33
eventus 98
evertere 81
evocare 84
ex 2
excedere 66
excellere 89
excipere 27
excitare 46
excludere 74
excusare 77
excutere 78
exemplum 29
exercere 14
exercitus 16
exhaurire 89
exigere 35
exiguus 93
exilium 66
eximere 60
eximius 95
exire 20
existimare 15
existimatio 67
exitium 70
exitus 72
exoriri 97
expedire 36
expellere 61
experiri 49
expers 87
expetere 71

explere 98
explicare 60
explorare 68
exponere 43
exprimere 51
expugnare 77
exquirere 99
exsequi 99
exspectare 18
exspectatio 83
exstinguere 89
externus 60
extra 79
extremus 42
exuere 87

facere 2
facies 39
facilis 11.
facinus 37
factum 12
facultas 50
fallere 21
falsus 92
fama 13
fames 55
familia 25
familiaris 28
familiaritas 86
fari 16
fas 91
fastigium 91
fatalis 93
fateri 33
fatigo 84
fatum 36
fauces 99
favere 64
favor 78
fax 39

felix 69
femina 43
fere 89
ferire 64
ferme 89
ferox 61
ferre 4
ferreus 86
ferrum 14
ferus 31
fessus 58
festinare 74
festus 98
fidelis 72
fidere 37
fides 13
fiducia 95
fidus 42
fieri 5
figere 41
figura 78
filia 20
filius 8
fingere 31
finire 48
finis 18
finitimus 91
firmare 50
firmus 47
flagitare 82
flagitium 45
flagrare 88
flamma 41
flare 93
flavus 95
flectere 56
flere 49
florere 53
fluctus 50
fluere 78

flumen 21
fluvius 59
focus 96
fodere 77
foedare 61
foedus 26
folium 100
fons 43
foris 36
forma 53
formare 66
formido 77
fors 19
fortis 12
fortuna 12
forum 29
fovere 81
frangere 38
frater 11
fraus 55
fremere 67
frequens 48
frequentare 95
fretum 95
fretus 69
frons 33
fructus 78
frui 49
frumentarius 89
frumentum 29
frustra 76
fuga 26
fugare 40
fugere 15
fulgere 92
fulmen 66
fundare 34
fundus 73
fungi 84
funis 97

funus 50
furere 49
furor 38
furtum 62

gaudere 28
gaudium 50
gelidus 100
gemere 74
geminus 75
gener 22
generare 95
genjtor 77
gens 11
genu 29
genus 13
gerere 9
germanus 65
gestare 70
gignare 65
gladiator 76
gladius 65
gloria 22
gloriari 50
gradus 47
grandis 75
gratia 11
gratulari 90
gratus 18
gravare 70
gravis 12
gravitas 60
grex 95

habere 2
habitare 37
habitus 77
haec 1
haerere 48
harena 61

hasta 42
haud 11
haurire 69
herba 46
hereditas 90
heres 63
heus 97
hic 1
hiems 58
hinc 11
hoc 1
hodie 19
homo 3
honestum 74
honestus 30
honor 15
honorare 42
hora 54
horrere 63
horridus 97
hortari 71
hospes 40
hospitium 58
hostilis 59
hostis 5
huc 3
humanitas 58
humanus 60
humus 61

iacere (iaceo) 30
iacere (iacio) 43
iactare 39
iam 2
ianua 91
ibi 12
ictus 53
id 1
idcirco 69
idem 4

ideo 16
idoneus 67
idus 51
igitur 9
ignarus 44
ignavus 97
ignis 19
ignominia 70
ignorare 45
ignoscere 39
ignotus 90
ille 1
illic 4
illico 79
illustris 70
imago 38
imber 73
imitari 97
immanis 68
immensus 78
imminere 84
immortalis 44
impedimentum 79
impedire 34
impellere 61
imperare 25
imperator 21
imperitus 87
imperium 9
impetrare 39
impetus 23
impius 85
implere 64
implorare 87
imponere 40
improbus 32
impudens 78
impurus 51
imus 79
in 1

inanis 65
incedere 54
incendere 64
incendium 53
incertus 48
incidere 41
incipere 32
incitare 74
inclinare 82
includere 65
incolumis 56
incredibilis 54
increpare 73
incumbere 97
inde 24
indicare 28
indicium 56
indignus 42
inducere 36
induere 80
indulgere 58
industrius 91
inermis 93
iners 85
inesse 74
infamis 100
infelix 49
infensus 85
inferre 25
inferus 52
infestus 61
infimus 75
infinitus 98
ingenium 18
ingens 17
ingratus 70
ingredii 49
inimicitia 72
inimicus 22
iniquus 45

inire 38
initium 42
iniuria 33
innocens 59
inopia 60
inops 83
insanus 83
insequi 46
insidiae 40
insidiari 91
insigne 66
insignis 55
instare 41
instituere 28
institutum 85
instruere 44
insula 34
insuper 73
integer 30
intellegere 9
intendere 59
inter 5
intercedere 75
interdum 56
interea 36
interesse 34
interficere 52
interim 40
interimere 71
interire 57
interponere 79
interrogare 62
intra 67
intrare 39
intro 35
invadere 57
invenire 14
invidere 55
invidia 27
invidiosus 100

invitare 68
invitus 38
ipsa 2
ipse 2
ipsum 2
ira 19
iracundia 90
irasci 33
ire 2
irridere 93
irritus 88
irrumpere 91
is 1
ista 3
iste 3
istud 3
ita 4
itaque 22
item 43
iter 18
iterum 37
iubere 6
iucundus 51
iudex 13
iudicare 10
iudicium 8
iungere 31
iurare 37
ius 8
iussum 36
iustus 40
iuvare 31
iuvenis 22
iuventa 85
iuventus 49
iuxta 43

labi 47
labor 21
laborare 28

lacessere 83
lacrima 32
lacrimare 82
lacus 61
laedere 44
laetari 96
laetitia 63
laetus 33
laevus 88
lapis 72
largitio 91
latitudo 39
latro 98
latrocinium 98
latus (adj.) 51
latus (n.) 52
laudare 18
laus 19
lavare 64
lectus 79
legare 10
legatio 52
legatus 31
legere 14
legio 9
lenire 88
lenis 92
leno 55
lentus 87
leo 91
lepidus 54
letum 95
levare 49
levis 24
lex 9
libare 41
libellus 95
liber (adj.) 26
liber (m.) 47
liberalis 87

liberalitas 87
liberare 27
liberi 59
libertas 20
libet 30
libido 35
librare 90
licentia 85
liceri 26
licet 24
lignum 86
limen 62
lingua 38
linquere 90
littera 6
litus 20
locare 16
locus 6
longitudo 82
longus 7
loqui 10
lucere 80
lucrum 91
luctus 83
lucus 47
ludere 43
ludus 37
lugere 58
lumen 36
luna 83
lupus 83
lux 32

machina 96
maeror 96
maestus 68
magis 15
magister 48
magistratus 30
magnitudo 32

magnus 2
mala 56
malle 21
malum 14
malus 11
manare 58
mandare 31
mandatum 83
manere 20
manes 50
manifestus 86
manus 7
mare 34
maritus 69
mater 10
materia 75
materibus 84
matrimonium 67
maturus 92
maximus 18
mediocris 89
meditari 93
medium 40
medius 22
membrum 63
memini 29
memor 37
memorare 37
memoria 28
mens 17
mensis 52
mentiri 62
merces 63
merere 29
meritum 72
metiri 69
metuere 23
metus 14
meus 3
miles 7

militare 26	movere 12	negotium 22
militaris 67	mox 20	nemo 10
militia 47	mulier 22	nempe 75
mille 17	multitudo 20	nemus 71
minae 80	multo 15	nepos 53
minari 81	multus 3	neque 2
minimus 58	mundus 100	nequiquam 65
minister 85	municipium 56	nequire 5
minor 97	munire 66	nescire 28
minuere 69	munitio 64	nescius 49
mirari 51	munus 23	neu 75
mirus 47	murmur 99	neuter 83
miscere 34	murus 27	neve 75
miser 16	mutare 24	niger 96
miseria 73		nihil 3
misericordia 65	nam 2	nil 3
missus 90	nancisci 67	nimis 44
mitis 80	nare 56	nimius 41
mittere 6	narrare 36	nisi 9
modestus 98	nasci 20	niti 8
modo 7	natare 75	nobilis 25
modus 4	natio 46	nobilitas 80
moenia 40	natura 16	nocere 39
moles 81	natus 26	nocturnus 69
molestus 40	nauta 80	nolle 15
mollire 96	navare 55	nomen 6
mollis 81	navigare 57	nominare 26
monere 32	navis 19	non 1
mons 16	ne 6	nondum 35
monstrare 72	nec 2	nonus 100
monstrum 83	necare 52	nos 4
monumentum 55	necessarius 40	noscere 16
mora 57	necesse 26	noster 3
morari 35	necessitas 43	nota 90
morbus 52	necessitudo 62	notus 50
mori 20	nefarius 77	novare 34
mors 10	nefas 74	novem 91
mortalis 51	negare 13	novus 16
mos 13	neglegere 45	nox 10
motus 67	negotior 78	nubere 63

nubes 97
nudare 77
nudus 58
nullus 3
num 50
numen 24
numerus 16
nummus 39
numquam 11
nunc 3
nuntiare 26
nuntius 47
nuper 45
nuptiae 53
nusquam 67
nympha 89

ob 12
obesse 97
obicere 61
obire 69
oblivisci 47
obruere 87
obscurus 77
obsecrare 34
observare 61
obsidio 92
obstare 63
obtinere 37
obvius 56
occasio 55
occidere 26
occulare 67
occupare 33
occurrere 47
octavus 99
octo 98
oculus 12
odi 51
odium 24

offendere 44
officium 20
olim 31
omen 55
omittere 32
omnino 30
omnis 3
onerare 75
onus 50
opera 18
operire 82
opinari 36
opinio 38
oportet 15
opperiri 96
oppido 92
oppidum 21
opponere 80
opportunus 97
opprimere 38
oppugnare 46
ops 20
optare 30
optimus 39
opus 8
ora 49
oraculum 89
orare 19
oratio 15
orator 48
orbis 59
ordiri 61
ordo 13
origo 48
oriri 26
ornamentum 53
ornare 24
ornatus 93
ortus 92
os (oris) 34

os (ossis) 59
ostendere 11
ostium 78
otiosus 100
otium 46

paene 31
palam 90
palma 97
par 31
parare 13
paratus 100
parcere 53
parens 35
parere (pareo) 25
parere (pario) 46
paries 62
pariter 82
pars 4
partire 91
partiri 92
partus 85
parum 69
parvus 5
pascere 71
passim 68
passus 58
pastor 94
patefacere 81
pater 4
patere 35
paternus 58
pati 12
patria 30
patricius 71
patrius 22
patruus 80
paucus 31
paulatim 73
paulum 39

paulus 37
pauper 97
pavidus 95
pavor 81
pax 13
peccare 54
pectus 17
pecunia 10
pecus 40
pelagus 86
pellere 34
pendere (pendeo) 68
pendere (pendo) 62
penetrare 97
penitus 60
penna 85
per 2
peragere 69
percellere 92
percutere 73
perdere 18
perducere 80
peregrinus 92
perferre 35
perficere 30
perfidia 92
pergere 48
periculosus 89
periculum 10
perire 14
peritus 100
permanere 87
permittere 44
pernicies 89
perpetuus 58
perscribere 68
persequi 48
persona 91

perspicere 44
persuadere 59
perterrere 88
pertimescere 80
pertinere 25
perturbare 79
pervenire 26
pes 43
pestis 74
petere 6
petitio 84
pietas 44
pingere 57
piscis 88
pius 52
placare 35
placere 17
placidus 76
planus 50
plaudere 90
plebs 13
plenus 30
plurimus 51
poculum 90
poena 18
poeta 42
polliceri 55
pondus 48
ponere 8
pontus 56
popularis 98
populare 27
populus 4
porrigere 99
porta 31
portare 45
porticus 84
portus 32
poscere 28
posse 2

possessio 62
possidere 92
post 7
postea 17
posterus 23
posthac 74
postquam 18
postridie 86
postulare 19
potare 27
potens 57
potentia 78
potestas 14
potiri 72
potis 7
prae 64
praebere 39
praeceps 75
praecipere 48
praecipitare 68
praecipuus 66
praeclarus 47
praeda 22
praedicare 39
praeditus 97
praedium 84
praedo 75
praeesse 48
praefectus 84
praeferre 76
praeficere 49
praemittere 71
praemium 30
praeponere 86
praesens 26
praesentia 95
praesentire 92
praesertim 31
praesidium 17
praestare (adv.) 40

praestare 43
praeter 20
praeterea 32
praeterire 40
praetermittere 63
praetor 17
praetorius 73
precari 79
premere 32
pretium 44
prex 40
pridem 65
pridie 82
primo 34
primus 5
princeps 15
principium 66
prior 10
priscus 96
pristinus 89
privare 32
privatim 99
privatus 57
pro 3
probare 18
procedere 40
procul 30
prodere 47
prodesse 52
prodire 83
producere 52
proelium 23
profecto 77
proferre 38
proficere 28
proficisci 25
profiteri 68
profugere 98
progredi 84
prohibere 26

proinde 76
proles 85
promittere 34
pronuntiare 82
pronus 97
prope 23
properare 46
properus 71
propinquus 67
proponere 44
proprius 36
propter 9
propterea 71
prosequi 76
prospicere 73
protinus 76
providere 53
provincia 9
proximus 40
prudens 58
publicare 34
publicus 8
pudere 51
pudor 34
puella 30
puer 14
pugna 23
pugnare 19
pulcher 37
pulsare 85
pulvis 92
puppis 74
purgare 78
purpureus 86
putare 5

quae 1
quaerere 7
quaeso 28
quaestio 61

quaestor 50
quaestus 67
qualis 49
quam 2
quamquam 43
quamvis 53
quando 24
quantus 10
quartus 77
quasi 9
quatere 100
quattuor 41
que 16
querela 83
queri 34
qui 1
quia 4
quicumque 27
quid 1
quidam 6
quidem 3
quies 64
quiescere 45
quin 8
quinque 32
quintus 39
quippe 43
quire 37
quis 1
quisquam 6
quisque 7
quisquis 14
quivis 31
quo 5
quoad 68
quod 1
quondam 36
quoniam 14
quoque 16
quot 60

quotiens 44

radius 98
radix 100
ramus 63
rapere 30
rapidus 93
rarus 45
ratio 7
ratis 76
recedere 60
recens 36
recipere 16
recordari 85
recusare 52
reddere 12
redigere 80
redire 7
reditus 88
reducere 52
referre 8
reficere 6
regere 16
regina 63
regio 36
regius 38
regnare 33
regnum 21
reicere 87
religio 22
religiosus 82
relinquere 8
reliquiae 89
reliquus 22
remanere 88
remittere 35
removere 46
remus 70
renuntiare 83
repellere 76

repentinus 80
reperire 25
repetere 34
reprehendere 47
repudiare 99
requirere 50
reri 5
res 2
rescribere 71
reservare 83
resistere 57
respicere 48
respondere 14
responsum 98
restare 46
restituere 33
retinere 24
retro 99
reus 12
revertere 32
revocare 38
rex 10
ridere 61
ripa 47
robur 58
rogare 16
rogatio 92
rogitare 88
rogus 90
rostrum 81
rota 93
ruere 44
ruina 82
rumor 57
rumpere 57
rursus 38
rus 12
rusticus 94

sacer 27

sacerdos 39
sacrare 41
sacrificium 76
saeculum 76
saepe 35
saevire 71
saevitia 86
saevus 39
sagitta 76
saltem 85
saltus 73
salus 15
salutare 37
salvus 34
sancire 43
sanguis 19
sanus 11
sapere 34
sapiens 98
sapientia 80
satis 83
saxum 27
scaena 94
scelerare 87
scelus 23
scientia 94
scilicet 21
scire 5
scribere 5
scutum 81
se 2
secare 81
secernere 65
secundo 85
secundum 60
secundus 28
securis 92
securus 72
secus 88
sed 1

sedare 53
sedes 52
seditio 44
segnis 79
semel 47
semper 9
senator 44
senatus 4
senectus 67
senex 21
sensus 63
sententia 12
sentire 11
sepelire 84
septem 67.
septimus 70
sepulcrum 77
sequi 7
serere 51
sero 25
serus 94
servare 16
servire 34
servitium 94
servitus 62
servus 20
sese 2
seu 11
severitas 71
severus 68
sex 33
sextus 64
si 1
sic 4
sicut 16
sidus 41
signare 30
significare 20
significatio 96
signum 15

silentium 61
silere 62
silva 23
similis 24
similitudo 81
simul 10
simulacrum 58
simulare 53
simulatio 100
sin 53
sine 22
sinere 11
singularis 44
sinister 93
sinus 54
sistere 92
sive 11
socer 79
societas 42
socius 28
sodalis 94
sol 18
solacium 89
solere 13
solitudo 94
sollicitare 73
sollicitus 81
solum (*adv.*) 29
solum (*m.*) 59
solus 12
solvere 26
somnus 36
sonare 43
sonus 90
sordidus 96
soror 23
sors 38
spargere 55
spatiari 70
spatium 31

species 30
spectaculum 60
spectare 22
sperare 18
spernere 60
spes 9
spiritus 66
splendor 83
spoliare 53
spolium 80
sponte 51
stare 8
statim 21
statio 67
statua 63
statuere 23
stella 92
sternere 68
stipendium 88
stirps 76
stringere 88
struere 74
studere 82
studiosus 79
studium 12
stultus 46
stuprum 91
suadere 56
sub 10
subigere 79
subire 21
subitus 54
submittere 98
subsidium 59
subvenire 78
succedere 51
sufferre 72
sufficere 72
sumere 18
summa 38

summus 23
super 69
superare 32
superbia 93
superbus 56
superesse 57
superus 9
supplex 70
supplicium 36
supra 51
surgere 54
sus 31
suscipere 27
suspendere 69
suspicari 50
sustentare 99
sustinere 26
suus 4

tabella 81
tabula 33
tacere 21
talentum 100
talis 17
tam 5
tamen 3
tametsi 79
tamquam 25
tandem 24
tangere 28
tantus 3
tardo 99
tardus 55
taurus 59
tectum 45
tegere 20
tela 52
tellus 46
telum 27
temere 64

temeritas 84
tempestas 13
templum 17
tempus 4
tendere 35
tener 52
tenere 7
tenuis 77
ter 57
terere 59
tergum 37
terra 8
terrere 47
terror 37
tertius 29
testamentum 70
testis 32
theatrum 70
timere 15
timidus 64
timor 29
toga 84
tolerare 99
tollere 15
tormentum 87
torquere 62
tot 19
totidem 82
totus 6
trabs 93
tractare 59
tradere 14
traducere 82
trahere 24
trans 88
transferre 42
transigere 89
transire 25
tremere 94
trepidare 82

trepidus 76
tres 17
tribuere 42
tribunus 10
tribus 56
triginta 86
tristis 45
triumphare 66
triumphus 48
trucidare 94
tu 1
tueri 16
tum 4
tumultus 51
tumulus 78
tunc 24
turba 51
turbare 26
turbo 26
turma 96
turpis 43
turpitudo 96
turris 60
tutor 95
tutus 62
tuus 2
tyrannus 81

uber 86
ubi 5
ubique 71
ulcisci 62
ullus 10
ultimus 50
ultra 81
ultro 63
umbra 45
umbrare 86
umerus 65
umquam 17

unda 30
undare 64
undique 45
unicus 88
universus 47
unus 4
urbanus 55
urbs 4
urere 79
urgere 55
usquam 79
usque 19
usurpare 83
usus 26
ut 1
uter 12
uti 9
utilitas 62
utinam 49
uxor 15

vacare 72
vacuus 78
vadere 89
vagus 98
valere 11
valetudo 75
validus 21
valles 83
vallum 90
vanus 96
varietas 86
varius 47
vastare 66
vastus 96
vates 59
vehemens 55
vehere 64
vel 4
velare 71

velle 3
vellere 29
velox 100
velum 75
velut 24
vena 89
vendere 33
venenum 57
venerari 96
venia 59
venire 3
ventus 35
venus 84
verberare 79
verbum 7
vereri 28
veritas 88
vero 13
verrere 41
versare 41
versus 68
vertere 18
vertex 66
verus 6
vester 8
vestigium 46
vestire 90
vestis 32
vetare 28
veteranus 74
vetus 25
vetustas 74
vetustus 88
vexare 74
via 20
vicinus 67
vicis 53
victor 23
victoria 19
victus 100

vicus 94
videlicet 99
videre 2
vigilare 72
vigilia 88
viginti 62
vilis 85
villa 70
vincere 13
vincire 57
vindicare 69
vinum 62
violare 65
vir 7
virere 67
virga 72
virgo 24
virilis 94
virtus 8
vis 7
visere 29
visum 64
visus 79
vita 11
vitare 24
vitium 41
vitta 100
vivere 11
vivus 54
vix 20
vocare 8
volumen 100
voluntas 21
voluptas 37
volvere 23
vos 2
vox 12
vulgare 77
vulgus 42
vulnerare 54

English Index

abandon 8
able to, be 2, 37
about 88, 93
above 51, 69, 73
above, be 57
absent, be 15, 21
abundance 14
accept 5
access 82
accident 36
accompany 76, 94
accomplish 23, 30, 39, 99
according to 3
account 7
accusation 15
accuse 29, 52
accustomed to, be 13
acknowledge 76
acquire 67,72,93
across 88
act energetically 55
act savagely 71
active 91
active service 47
actually 4,21
adapt to 86
add 56
add on 56
address 13
admire 83
admit 33,54,72
admonish 55
adolescent 29
adorned 93
adornment 53
adultery 98
advance 28,38,51
advantageous, be 52
advise 32,56

affect 39
affection 97
afraid, be 15
afraid, be very 80
after 7, 18, 60
after this 74
afterwards 17
again 37, 38
against 8
age 13,73,74
aggressive 61
agitate 43,73
agitated 76,81
agree 17,44
agreeable 18,51,76
agreement 31,65
aid 31,59,78
air 42,65,68
alas! 83
alike 82
alive 54
all 3,6,29
alleviate 88
allied 28
allot 42
allow 11
allure 84
ally 28
almost 31,89
alone 7,29
along 2
already 2
also 1,16,43
altar 41
alter 24,93
alternatively 53
although 23,43,53, 79
altogether 30
always 9

ambassador 31
ambition 36
ambush 40,91
among 5
ample 20
ancient 25,31,88,96
and 1,16
and not 75
anger 19,90
angry 85
angry, be 33
announce 26, 28
annoy 74
annoying 40
another 4
answer 14,98
anticipate 48,73
antique 96
antiquity 74
any 10
anybody 6
anyone 10
anything 6,10
anywhere 79
apartment block 34
apparent, be 25.
appear 53,83
appearance 39, 77
appoint 94
appoint as envoy 10
approach 18,65,82
appropriate 42,67, 97
approve 18,95
apt 50
arch 49,75
argue 52,82
argument 55
arm 12,60
army 16

around 88,93
arouse 39,65
arrange 28,56,59, 69,74,81
arrival 55
arrive 22,26
arrogance 93
arrogant 56
arrow 76
art 32
as 1
as far as 19
as if 9,24,25
as long as 36
as much as you please 53
ashamed, be 51
ashes 87
ask 16
ask for 19, 28
ask frequently 88
asking 92
assault 46
assemble 71
assembly 81
assent 8
association 42
astonished, be 51
at 1,5
at every point 19
at first 34
at last 17,24
at least 85
at once 21
at the same time 10, 82
at, be 11
attack 23,46, 57,6, 62,65,84,97
attendant 58,85

augur 91
augury 65
august 49
author 24
authority 9,13
avarice 68
avenge 6 2,69
avert 41
avoid 24
awake, be 72
awaken 46
awareness 99
away, be 15
axe 92
axis 99
back 37
backwards 99
bad 11,32
baggage 79
balance, keep in 90
banishment 66
banquet 54,91
barbarian 72
bare 58,77
base 59,73
bathe 64
battle 23,23
battle line 22
battlements 80
be 1
be green 67
be healthy 11
be in 74
be in the way 97
be mad 49
beach 61
beak 81
beam 93
bear 4, 70
beat 68,79,85,90

beautiful 37
beauty 74
because 4,14
because of 9 ,12 ,64
bed 79
befall 27
before 3 ,5 ,29 ,64
before, be 48
beg 19,19,28,79
beg for 34
begin 18,32,61
beginning 42,66
beginning, in the 34
behind 7 ,60,99
behold 32
belief 13,38
believe 6, 37
below 52
bend 54, 56,82
beneath 10
benefit 24
benefit from 49
benevolence 80
bequeath 10
beseech 34
besides 32,63
best 39
betray 14,47
between 5
between, be 34
beware 37
beyond 20,69, 79,81
bid for 26
big 2
bind 57
bird 73
birth 13,26,46,85, 92
bitter 59,66
black 54,96
blame 4 3,47

blessed 92
blind 97
block 34
blockade 65,92
blood 19,81
bloodshed 19,81
bloom 53
blow 53,93
board 33,81
boast of 50
boat 19
body 9
bold 59
boldness 40
bond 62
bone 59
book 59,100
booklet 95
booty 22,80
border 49
born, be 20
both 12,45
bottom 59
boundary 18,36
bow 49,75
boy 14
branch 63
brandish 90
breadth 39
break 38, 57
break out 78
break up 26
breath 66
breathing 66
breeze 65
brief 45
bright 21,70
brightness 83
brilliant 47
bring 4

bring across 82
bring back 8, 52
bring down 22, 30
bring forth 22,38,65
bring out 46,47
bring over 80
bring to 14, 27,81
bring together 14,
23, 27,40,90
bristle 63
broad 51
brother 11
brow 33
build 74,82
building 61
bull 59,60
burden 50 ,70,75
burn 33,64,79,88
burning 81
burst in 91
burst out 78
bury 84
business 2,7, 22
business, be in 78
but 1 ,3 ,6 ,7
but if 53
buy 51
by 1 ,2 ,5
by a little 39
by much 15
call 8 ,13,91
call out 84
calm down 53
camp 17
can 2,37
capable 7,5 7
capitulation 85
captivate 56
captive 75
capture 77

care 14
care for 12
careful 63
careful, be 37
carefulness 71
carry 4,9,45,64,70
carry away 25
carry before 76
carry in 25
carry through 35
carry to 14
castle 68
catch 47,85
cause 3,66
cavalry 77
cavalryman 17
cave 92
cease 53,69
celebrate 50
celestial 84
censor 73
central 22
centurion 38
century 76
certain 6
certain person, thing
6
certainly 21,77
chance 12,19
change 18,24,93
channel 95
character 13,18
chariot 48
charm 84
charming 54
cheap 85
cheat 6 7,77
cheek 56
chest 17
children 47

countryside 12
courage 8,40
course 51
cover 20,67,71,82 , 87
cow 60
craft 32
crass 80
create 29,31,65,95
crime 15,23,37
crisis 45
crowd 21,51
crowd together 50, 95
crowded 44,48
crown 64,87
cruel 41,64
cruelty 61
crush 32,94
cry 29,49,82
cultivate 22
cultivated 99
cultivation 99
cup 90
curia 44
curtain 75
curve 54
custody 64
custom 13, 30
cut 81
cut down 23,26
daily 93
danger 10,89
dangerous 89
dare 19
daring 59
dark 54,77
daughter 20, 30
day 5
daylight 32

dear 41
dearness 97
death 10,50,95
debauchery 91
deceit 57
deceive 21,67
deception 55
decide 10,21
decision 71,73,80
declare 70,84
decorate 24
decorated 93
decoration 53,66
decree 7 3,80
dedicate 84
deed 12
deep 37
defection 96
defence 50
defend 12
defendant 12
defender 91
definite 6
deify 86
delay 35,57,99
deliberate 11
delight 58
demand 19, 28,82
demand again 34
demonstrate 56
den 92
denounce 82
dense 4 4,68
deny 13,96
depart 24, 25
departure 72
deprive of 32
descend 54
descendant 53
descendants 85

describe 86
desert 36
deserve 29
deserving 22
desire 18,35,36,37, 46,70,71,77
desiring 46
despair 77.
despise 40
despoil 53
destiny 36
destroy 57, 59,70, 71,84,98
destruction 53,70, 82,89
deter 90
determine 78
devastate 27
devastated 96
device 96
devote 10
devoted to, be 64
dialect 38
dictator 29
die 14,20,20,57,69
differ 48
different, be 34
difficult 50,99
difficulty 96
dig 77
dignify 42
diligence 71
diligent 63
diminish 69
dire 78
direct 16,32,59
dirty 96
disagreement 69
disaster 53, 54,74
discern 33,34

discipline 43
discourage 90
discover 14,70
discuss 82
disease 52
disgrace 45,70,95 , 96
disgraceful 26
disguise 66
dishonour 61,95
dismiss 23,31
dispatch 63
disperse 24
display 11
dispute 57
dissension 44,69
dissolve 84
distance, at a 30
distinguished 50,95
distribute 81
district 94
disturb 26, 39, 73
divide 43 ,91,92
divination 42
divine 19,73
divine law 91
divine will 24
division 45
do 2,3,40
do something to 39
dog 86
domestic 62
dominate 32, 38
donate 33
door 36,91
doorway 78,91
double 77
doubt 19
doubtful 33
down from 1

drag 24,59
drain 6 9,89
draw 19
draw back 16, 52
draw tight 88
dread 14,29
drink 27,61
drip 58
drive 3,13,73
drive away 34
drive back 7 6,80
drive off 79
drive out 35,61
drive to 94
drive under 79
drop 72
drug 57
during 2
dust 92
dutiful 52
duty 20,23
dwell 37
each 7
each of two 12
eager 79
eager, be 82
eagerness 81
ear 28
earn 29
earth 8,46,59,61
easy 11
eddy 66
edge 22
effect 23
effort 18
eight 98
eighth 99
either 2
eject 48,69
elicit 84

embassy 52
embrace 6 8,88
eminent 55
emperor 21
empty 65,78,96,96
empty, be 72
encircle 78
enclose 65
encourage 71
end 18,42,69,72
endless 98
endowed with 97
endure 12,99
enemy 5
engage 89
enjoy 49
enjoyment 78
enmity 72
enormous 32
enough 83
enrol 51
enter 38,39,49
enthusiasm 12
entice out 84
entire 30,47
entirely 30,60
entrance 78
entreat 82
entreaty 36,40
entrust 31,38
envious 100
envy 27,55
equal 27,31,93
equalise 45
equestrian order 77
equip 12
era 76
erect 60
error 58
escape 98

especially 31
establish 23,28,35, 39,98
established 65
estate 42,70,84
esteem 14
estimate 6 6,69
estimation 67
eternal 72
eternity 73
evade 66
evaluate 15
even 2, 9
evenness 80
event 36, 98
ever 17
everlasting 44
every 7
everywhere 71
evidence 56
evident 86
evil 11,14,23,74
exact 35
examine 44
example 29
exceed 66
excel 43,89
excellent 57
except 9
exceptional 95
excessive 41
excessively 44
excite 60
exclude 74
excuse 77
exercise 14
exhaust 89
exhausted 58
exile 66
exist 15

exit 72
expect 18,96
expectation 83
expedient, be 36
expel 61,69,79
experience 49
expert 100
explain 60, 70
explicitly 90
explore 68
expose 43
express 51,74
expression 25
extend 59
extinguish 89
extraordinary 47
extreme 42
eye 12
face 25,34,39
face to face 89
faculty 50
fail 21,58,99
fair 27
fairness 80
faith 13
faithful 42,72
fall 17,27,36,99
fall on 41
false 92
fame 13,2 2 ,8 0
familiar 28
familiarity 86
family name 91
famine 55
famous 21,100
far away 30
farm 73
farmer 7 9,89
farthest 50
fashion 66

fast 100
fasten 41
fat 80
fatal 93
fate 3 6,38
fated 93
father 4,7 7
father-in-law 79
fatherly 22, 58
fault 41,43
favour 11, 24,64,78
fear 14,15,23,28,29, 37,77,81
fearful 6 4,76
fearful, be 82
feast 91
feather 85
feed 71
feel 11
feel beforehand 92
feeling 12,63
female 43
ferocity 86
festive 98
few 31
field 10,28
fifth 39
fight 19,23,23,26,58
fill up 64,72,98
filthy 26
finally 17,24,98
find 14,25
find out 70
finger 61
finish 30, 40,48, 69, 89 ,94
fire 19,53
fireplace 96
firmness 78
first 5,10

fish 88
fitting 42
five 32
fix 41
flame 41
flank 52
flat 50,93
flat surface 41
flee 15,73,88,98
fleet 25
flesh 71
flight 26
flock 40, 95
flourish 53
flow 58,78
flower 53
follow 7,67,76,99
follow after 46
follow up 48.
following 23, 28
food 70,100
foolish 46
foot 43
footprint 46
for 2, 3
for sure 43
for that reason 69
forbid 28
force 7,23,78
forehead 33
foreign 60,72 ,92
foreigner 5, 5,40
foresee 73
forest 23,71
forget 47
form 53,78
former 89
formerly 29
fort 17,68
fortification 27,90

fortifications 40
fortify 66,76
fortifying 64
fortress 42
fortunate 69
fortune 12
forum 29
foster 81
foul 26,43
found 15, 39
foundation 73
four 41
fourth 77
fraud 55,57
free 26
free from 78
free from, be 72
freedom 20
frequent 48,95
fresh 36
friend 9
friendly 9
friendship 27,86
frighten 47
frightened 95
from 1 ,1 ,2
from here 11
from there 24
front 33
fruitful 86
fulfil 6 4,98
full 30
funeral 50
funeral pile 90
furious 55
furthermore 63
gain 67,91
game 37
gate 31,84
general 21,35

generation 76
generosity 87
generous 85
gentle 80,81,92
get 39,67
get to know 16
get up 54
ghosts 50
gift 23,45
girl 30
give 3
give back 12
give birth 46
give out 22
give up 10,77
gladiator 76
glide 47
glorious 30
glory 22,55
glory in 50
glow 33
go 2,54 ,83,89
go again 34
go around 94
go away 13,54,66
go back 7
go between 75
go beyond 25
go in 57
go into 97
go out 20,43,66
go to 65,69
go under 21
god 5
goddess 34
godless 85
godlike 73
gold 13
golden 95
good 5

goodwill 11,78,80
gossip 57
grace 11
gradually 73
grain 29
grain supply 89
grand 17
grandchild 53
grandfather 60
grant 42
grasp 7,93 ,95
grasp at 56
grass 46
grateful 18
gratify 58
grave 77
gravity 60
great 2,75
greatest 18
greatly 15,92
greatness 32
greed 77
greedy 73
greet 37
grief 83,96
grieve 58
grieving 68
groan 67,74
ground 61
grove 47
grow 25,64
grow accustomed to 99
grow up 54,96
guard 16,17,42,82
guardian 95
guest 40
guild 87
habit 13,30
hail 37

hair 70,71
hand 7,9 7
hand over 14
hang 68,69
hang down 68
hang on to 48
happen 27,33,40, 41,47,5,54
happiness 63
happy 33,92
happy, be 96
harass 73
harbour 32
hard 50
harden 68
hardly 20
harm 39,44,44
harmless 59
harmony 65
harsh 65,66
hasty 71
hate 27,51
hating 100
hatred 24
have 2
hazardous 89
he 1
head 15
headlong 75
health 15,75
healthy 11,21,34,67
heap 81
hear 6
heart 85
hearth 96
heat 78,81
heaven 68
heavenly 84
heavens 30
heavy 12

height 46
heir 63
help 31,35,52,59, 74,90
hence 11
her 4
herb 46
herd 40,95
here and there 68
hereafter 74
herself 2, 2
hesitate 19
hey! 97
hi! 97
hide 39,64,67,82
high 37
higher 9
highest 23
highwayman 98
hill 72
himself 2, 2
hinder 63,97
hindrance 79
hire 23
his 4
hit 64,73 ,79,85,92
hither 3
hitherto 19
hold 2,37,7,98
hold back 24,26,65
hold out 99
hollow 90
holy 27,49
home 5
homeland 30
honest 87
honour 15,42,55
honourable 30
hope 9 ,18
horn 54

128

join 31,40,56
join together 33
joined 50
joining together 75
journey 18
joy 50,63
joyful, be 96
judge 10,13,15
judgment 8
jump 73
just 7,40
just as 16, 24, 25,76
just as many 82
just so far 31
justifiable 40
justified 40
keen 73
keep 46
keep away from 65
keep together 27
keep warm 81
kill 23,26,52,52,71
kind 13,18
kind, of such a 3,17, 49
kind, of what 49
kindly 85
king 10
knee 29
knight 17
knock 34,92
know 5,10
knowledge 94
knowledge of, having 66
known 50
lack 48
lacking 83,87
lacking, be 21
lacking in, be 48

lake 61
lame 74
land 8 ,4 6
language 38
large 2, 20,75
large number 20
largesse 91
largest 18
last 87
late 25,55,94
laugh 61
laugh at 93
law 8 ,9
lay waste 66
lazy 55 ,85,97
lead 19,48
lead away 30, 52
lead in 36
lead out 45
lead over 82
lead to 27
leader 14,15
leaf 100
leap 73
learn 49
learn about 10
leave 90
leave behind 8
left 88,93
leg 33
legate 31
legation 52
legion 9
leisure 46
leisure, at 100
length 82
lessen 69
lest 6
let go 6,32 ,44
let pass 63

letter 6,21
level 27,50,93
liberal 85,87
liberate 27
liberty 20
licence 85
lie 30,62
lie down on 97
life 11
lifetime 76
lift up 15,49,93
light 24,32,36
lighten 49
lightning 66
like 24,31
likeness 58,81
likewise 43,82
limb 33,63
limit 1 8,48,49
limping 74
line 13,36,97
linger 35
lion 91
listen 6
literature 6
little 5,31,37,93
little by little 73
live 11
live in 22
living 54
load 70,75
locate 8,15,16,23
location 6
loiter 99
loneliness 94
long 7
long ago 65
long for 46
long-lasting 100
look! 45,84

neighbouring 67,67, 91
neither 2
neither of two 83
nephew 53
never 11
nevertheless 79
new 16, 36
newly-wed 89
next 17,23
nice 54
night 10
nightwatch 88
nine 91
ninth 100
nobility 80
noble 25,71
noble character 87
nobody 3,10
nocturnal 69
nod 24
noise 51,57,90
nominate 26
none 3
no-one 3,10
nor 2 ,75
north pole 99
not 1,2,6,11
not at all 3,11
not long ago 63
not yet 35
note 6 8,90
nothing 3
notice 49
notorious 50
nourish 19,71
nourishment 100
novel 16
now 2, 3
nowhere 67

number 16
numerous 44
nuptials 53
nymph 89
oak 58
oar 70
odedient 35
obey 25
obscure 77
observe 16,61
obstacle 79
obtain 39,93
occasion 55
occasionally 56
occupy 33
occupy oneself 84
occur 41
ocean 86
offend 44,44
offer 39
office 9,20,23
offspring 85,85
often 35
oh no! 83
old 21,25,31,88
old age 67
old man 21
omen 55,83
omit 32,40,63
on account of 69
on all sides 45
on behalf of 3
on that account 16
on the following day 86
once 47
once upon a time 31, 36
one 4
one of two 8

one's own 36
only 7 ,1 2 ,2 9
open 27,60
open,be 35
openly 90
opinion 8 ,1 2 ,3 8
opportune 97
opportunity 55
oppose 61,63,80
opposed 49,69
opposing 56
opposite 8,49,74
oppress 38
or 2,4
or else 2
or even 4
or if 11
oracle 89
orator 48
order 6,13,25,31, 36,83
ordinary 89
organize 44
origin 16,48,66
other 4,17
other one, the 8
otherwise 35,88
ought 15
our 3
ours 3
out of 1,2
outcome 98
outside 60,79
outstanding 47, 57
over 51,88
over, be 32
overhang 84
overhead 73
overlook 39
overshadow 86

87,88
remainder 22
remains 89
remarkable 25, 55
remember 29, 37,85
remind 47, 55
remove 25,46,60,91
renew 34
renounce 83
repair 6
repel 12,76
report 8,83
reputation 13,67
request 6,40,84
require 50
resemblance 81
reserve 83
resist 46, 57
resound 43
respond 14
rest 17,22,45,64
rest on 97
restore 6,12,33
restrain 24,75,94
restrained 98
result 98
retain 27
return 7, 32,88
reveal 38,72,81
reverence 22
reverent 82
revolt 44, 58
reward 30,72
rewrite 71
ribbon 100
rich 59,86
ridicule 40,93
right 8 ,1 5 ,3 3
ripe 80,92
rise 26

rise in waves 64
rise up 97,97
rising 92
river 2 1 ,4 6 ,5 9
riverbank 47
road 20
roaming 98
roar 49,67
robber 75,98
robbery 98
rock 27
role 91
roll 23,100
Roman citizen,
relating to a 56
roof 45
root 100
rope 97
rotate 18
rough 65,97
rout 40
row 13
royal 38
rub 59
ruin 70,82
rule 16,33
rumour 13,57
run 28
run away 15
run together 57
run up to 47
running 51
rural 76,94
rush 41,44,46,74,89
rustic 76,94
sacred 27,98
sacrifice 76
sad 16 ,45,68
safe 34 ,56,62
safety 15

sail 57
sailor 80
same 4
same place 31
sample 29
sanctify 41
sanction 43
sand 61
savage 39
say 1,16
say often 97
say yes 8
scarcely 20
scared 95
scatter 48, 55
scattered 45
sea 34,41,56,86
seal 15
sea-shore 20
season 13
seat 52
second 28
secondly 85
secretly 63
secure 72
security 17
see 2 ,3 3 ,4 7
see ahead 53
see into 44
seek 6,7,50
seek out 68,71,99
seeking 61
seer 59,91
seize 8,30,56,60,76,
83,85,95
seizing 63
select 14,30,42, 54
sell 33
senate 4
senator 44

send 6
send ahead 34,71
send away 23,31
send back 35
send down 72
send headlong 68
send out 63
send to 72
sending 90
sense 11
sense of duty 44
sentence 44
separate 43,65
sepulchre 77
serious 12
seriousness 60
servant 85
serve 23, 34
service 20
servile 20
servitude 62,94
set 40
set free 27, 36
set loose 26
set on fire 79
set out 25,43,44
seven 67
seventh 70
several 80
severe 68
severity 71
shade 45
shadow 45
shaggy 97
shake 100
shake off 78
shame 34,45,95
shameful 42,43, 51
shameless 78
shape 31,66,78

share 91,92,96
sharp 28
she 1
shepherd 94
shield 81
shine 80,92
ship 19
shooting 90
shore 47
short 45
shoulder 65
shout 29,49
show 11,47, 56,60, 72
shudder 63
shut out 74
sick 65
sickness 52
side 52
siege 92
sigh 74
sight 30,79
sign 15,30,56,96
signify 20,30
silence 61
silent, be 21,62
silently 63
silver 24
similar 24
simulate 53
simulation 100.
sin 74
sin, commit a 54
since 1,14
sing 42,86
single 44
singular 44
sire 95
sister 23
sit 37

sit down 55
situation 6
six 33
sixth 64
size 32
skilful 87
skill 32
skilled in 100
sky 30,68
slaughter 29,94
slave 20
slavery 62,94
slavish 20
sleep 36,45,87
slender 77
slip 47
slow 55,79,87
sluggish 79
small 5,37,93
smaller 97
smallest 58
smash 57
smile at 61
shake 95
snatch 30
so 4 ,4 ,5
so far 5 ,9
so great 3
so large 3
so long 9
so many 19,44,60
so much 5
so that 1
so that not 8
society 42
soft 52,81,92
soften 96
soil 61
soldier 7
soldier, be a 26

sole 12,88
solitude 94
some 80
someday 31
someone 10
something 10
sometimes 56
son 8,14
song 35
son-in-law 22
soon 20
soothe 35,53,96
soothsayer 91
sordid 96
sorrow 16
sorrowful 68
soul 4, 29
sound 11,43,90
source 48
sovereignty 21
sow 51
space 31
spare 53
speak 1,10,16,19
speak out 74
speaker 48
speaker's platform 81
speaking 15
spear 27, 42
special 66
species 30
spectacle 60
speech 15,38
speed 71
spirit 4,29 ,66
splendour 83
spoil 61
spoils 80
spoke of a wheel 98
spontaneously 51

sport 37
spread about 48
spread out 68
spring 43
sprinkle 55
spur on 74
spurn 60
stab 89
stage 94
stalk 76
stand 8,92
stand by 80
stand on 41
standing 67
star 41,92
start 42
state 6
station 67
statue 38, 58,63
status 14
stay 20, 37
steady 65
steep 99
stem 76
step 47, 58
stern 68
stern of a ship 74
sternness 71
stick 72,98
stick to 48
stone 27,72
stooping 97
stop 15,53,55,57
storeroom 89
storm 13,58,73
strain 8
strait 95
strange 16,31,60 ,92
stranger 5,40
stream 46

strength 58
strengthen 50
stretch 35,99
stride 58
strike 23,34,53,64,
68,73,90,92
strike against 61
strip 53,77
strive 27,35,95
strong 12,21,47
struggle 26,58,95
struggle for 33
stupid 4 6,88
subdue 38,38,77
subject 79
submit 98
succeed 51
sudden 54,80
suffer 12,41,72
suffice 72
sufficient 83 1
suffuse 72
suitable 50,67,97
summer 69
summit 38,91
summon 84,91
sun 18
superstition 22
superstitious 82
suppliant 70
supply 14,40,72
support 19, 26,72,
78,99, 99
sure, to be 75
surge 64
surname 91
surrender 10,85
surround 66,77,78,87
survive 57
suspect 50

train 14
training 43
transfer 42
transport 22, 45,64
trap 40
tray 81
treachery 92
tree 35
tree-trunk 93
tremble 82,94
trembling 81,97
trial 8
tribe 11,56
tribune 10
trick 21,57
trifling 24
triumph 48
triumph, have a 66
troop 96
trouble 14
troublesome 40
true 6
truly 6,13,38,75,77
trust 6,13,37,95
trustworthy 42
truth 13,88
try 1 8 ,39,49
turn 18,23,41
turn around 32, 53
turn away 41
turn towards 32
turned towards 69
turpitude 96
twenty 62
twice 42
twig 72
twin 75
twist 62
two 7
two-fold 77

two-sided 100
tyranny 21
tyrant 81
udder 86
unable, be 5
unarmed 93
unavoidable 40
unaware 49
unbelievable 54
unbroken 63
uncertain 33,48
uncle 80
unclean 51
unconcerned 72
uncover 27,77
undecided 100
under 10
understand 9
undertake 27
undertaking 85
Underworld 50
unequal 45
uneven 45
unexpected 54,80
unfair 45
unfold 60
unfortunate 49
unfriendly 22
ungrateful 70
unhappy 49
unharmed 30, 56
union 75,93
unique 88
unite 27
universe 100
unknown 44,90
unless 9
unlucky 49,88,93
unoccupied 100
unrelated 31

unskilled 85,87
unsure 48
until 7, 36
unwilling 38
unwilling, be 15
unworthy 42
upper 9
uproar 51
upset 79
urban 55
urbane 55
urge 55
urge on 71
use 9,2 6
use, be of 28, 52
use sparingly 53
used to, be 13
usefulness 62
usurp 83
vacant 65
vain 96
valley 83
value 44
varied 47
variety 86
various 47
vast 17, 78
vehement 55
vein 89
venerate 96
very many 77
very much 53,92
veteran 74
vex 74
vice 41
victory 19
vigilance 88
villa 70
village 94
violate 65

Made in the USA
San Bernardino, CA
18 April 2018